# As If!

## THE NOT SO CLUELESS ALICIA SILVERSTONE

*Jason Rich*

BOULEVARD BOOKS, NEW YORK

AS IF!: THE NOT SO CLUELESS ALICIA SILVERSTONE

A Boulevard Book / published by arrangement with
the author

PRINTING HISTORY
Boulevard special sales edition / June 1997

The Putnam Berkley World Wide Web site address is
http://www.berkley.com

ISBN: 1-57297-360-9

BOULEVARD
Boulevard Books are published by
The Berkley Publishing Group, a member of Penguin Putnam Inc.,
200 Madison Avenue, New York, New York 10016.
BOULEVARD and its logo are trademarks belonging to
Berkley Publishing Corporation.

PRINTED IN THE UNITED STATES OF AMERICA

# contents

# acknowledgments

Thanks to Elizabeth Beier and Jennifer Lata at The Berkley Publishing Group for offering me the opportunity to write this book and seeing the megastar potential of Alicia Silverstone. I'd also like to thank everyone who assisted me in writing this book, especially: Alan Friedman, Nina Paskowitz, Mona May, Dennis Frausnick, Michael Hasz, Lynn Helmsteadt, and the folks at the International Locator, Inc.

For helping to gather many of the photos featured in this book, I'd like to acknowledge the work of celebrity photographer and photo editor Mark Ragonese.

My sincere gratitude also goes out to my two best friends, Mark Giordani and Ellen Bromfield, for their ongoing friendship and support.

While they did not directly contribute to this book, I'd like to thank everyone involved with Alicia's career, especially:

Carolyn Kessler, Elizabeth Much, Amy Heckerling, Scott Rudin, Joel Schumacher, Aerosmith, and Alicia's parents, for helping to make Alicia popular enough for me to write this unauthorized book about her.

Finally, I'd like to offer my sincere congratulations to Alicia Silverstone, who has worked very hard to make her dreams and goals come true. She deserves all of the success that she has thus far achieved, and like all of her fans around the world, I look forward to seeing everything that she accomplishes in the future.

# alicia silverstone
# fast facts

| | |
|---|---|
| Date of Birth: | October 4, 1976 |
| Astrological Sign: | Libra |
| Place of Birth: | San Francisco, California |
| Current Residence: | Los Angeles, California, and San Francisco, California |
| Eye Color: | Green |
| Hair Color: | Brown/Blond |
| Height: | 5'9" |
| Religion: | Jewish |
| Mother's Name: | Didi (Deirdre) Silverstone |
| Father's Name: | Monty Silverstone |
| Brother's Name: | David Silverstone |
| Dog's Name: | Sampson |
| First Major Acting Role: | Appeared in a Domino's Pizza commercial at age 14 |
| Acting Debut on Stage: | *Carol's Eve*—Met Theater, Los Angeles |
| First Music Video: | Aerosmith's "Cryin' "— "Best Video of All Time" (MTV) |
| Manager's Name: | Carolyn Kessler |
| Schools She Attended: | Crocker Middle School and San Mateo High School. |

She earned her G.E.D. (high school equivalency) and
  became emancipated at age 15.

Favorite Foods:                   Apricot baby food,
                                    Lucky Charms, and
                                    Cocoa Pebbles

Name of Alicia's
  Production Company:             First Kiss Productions

First Movie Alicia's
  Production Company
  Produced:                      *Excess Baggage*

Charities Alicia Works
  with:                          Last Chance for Animals,
                                    the Ark Trust, People for
                                    the Ethical Treatment of
                                    Animals


Addresses Fans Can Send Mail to:

Alicia Silverstone            Alicia Silverstone
First Kiss Productions        % Premiere Artists
Columbia Pictures               Agency
10202 W. Washington           8899 Beverly Blvd.
  Blvd.                        Suite 510
Capra Blvd., Suite 106        Los Angeles, CA 90048
Culver City, CA 90232

# introduction

## Who Is Alicia Silverstone?

So y'all wanna find out about Alicia Silverstone? Well, just a few short years ago, very few people knew who she was. Her fame and fortune has happened very quickly by Hollywood standards. These days, however, Alicia has become a household name, not only in America, but in many countries throughout the world.

Most of her fans know her as "Batgirl" from *Batman and Robin*, the star of *Clueless*, or the girl from the Aerosmith music videos, but as you'll quickly discover by reading this book, in the past few years Alicia has been very busy making a bunch of movies and working hard for several

1

charities to help protect all of the animals on our planet.

So, what sets Alicia apart from the many other young actresses in Hollywood? Well, most obviously, she's a total Betty (that's *Clueless*-talk for an attractive woman). She also happens to be a talented actress, not to mention an extremely motivated, likable, and down-to-earth person. On July 16, 1995, James Ryan, a writer for the *New York Times*, wrote, "Like most 18-year-olds, Alicia Silverstone seems to approach life with the naive fascination of a bear cub emerging from its den for the first time. In a town of 18-year-olds going on 35, she is 18 going on 18." Now Alicia is in her early twenties, and her philosophy toward life and drive for success haven't changed a bit!

Alicia is a very private person who works hard but tries to stay out of the public eye. While she is almost constantly going from one acting job to the next, with no break in between, what personal life she does have she considers her own—as if someone with her popularity could possibly have a normal life when she's not working. But who can blame her for trying?

While she has many male friends, she claims that she doesn't currently date. Many of the people she works with, along with her closest friends, respect her wish to remain private and refuse to talk about her in public.

When she's hanging around her house, Alicia says that she's a very casual and nonmaterialistic person who enjoys wearing sweatpants and her favorite T-shirt. She wears little or no makeup, and doesn't like getting dressed up in fancy clothes.

Recently, however, Alicia has been making appearances at major Hollywood events, like the Academy Awards, the MTV Movie Awards, and a bunch of charity events, but unless she happens to be promoting one of her latest movies (*Batman and Robin* or *Excess Baggage*), she does very few television, print, or radio interviews. When Alicia does happen to make a public appearance, she's almost always dressed in designer fashions, right down to her sunglasses. Like many of Hollywood's biggest stars, Alicia gets most of her sunglasses from a boutique called Optical Outlook in Beverly Hills, California. Alicia has been seen wearing designer Kata Luxus sunglasses in the avocado color, which have a retail price of around $350. "Alicia wears sunglasses from several top designers, including Kata and Isaac Mizrahi. They range in price from about a hundred fifty to three hundred fifty dollars," says a representative from Optical Outlook.

As you might have guessed, Alicia and her management weren't too thrilled to discover that this unauthorized biography was being written, and as a result provided no information or support to this project. The information in this book comes from interviews that Alicia has done over the past several years, and directly from people who have worked with her.

From this book, you'll get a good understanding of who Alicia is, because you'll be reading exclusive interviews with her acting teacher, along with her makeup artist, hair stylist, and costume designer from *Clueless*. From these interviews, you'll find out how you can follow the same hair and skin care regime as Alicia, and avoid being a fashion victim. This book offers detailed information about all of the major acting roles Alicia has had, plus facts about the movies she's starred in. You're about to find out what it was like for Alicia to both star in and coproduce *Excess Baggage*, and then star in the hottest movie of 1997—*Batman and Robin*.

This book also reveals information about what charities Alicia is active in supporting and how you too can help those charities.

Plus, you'll learn how to gather even more info about your favorite young actress by surfing the Internet's World Wide Web! Oh, and if you skip directly to the middle of the book, you'll find a section that's jam-packed with awesome photos of Alicia, many of which are exclusive. Thanks to Alan Friedman (the makeup artist from *Clueless*), this book also features the makeup test photos that Alan took while *Clueless* was in production, so you can see firsthand what types of makeup were used on Alicia, and how it changed her appearance from scene to scene.

Until Alicia became famous a few years ago, she led a totally normal life for a young girl growing up in California. She went to school, studied acting, and hung out with friends. She continues to be extremely close with her family. This book primarily focuses on Alicia's life after she became famous, but even though that has only been within the last few years, you'll see that she has accomplished an amazing amount in this relatively short time.

As you read this book, chill out, kick back, and get ready to find out just about everything you ever wanted to know about Alicia Silverstone!

# oNe

## Meet "A-lee-see-ah"

JUST ABOUT EVERY TEENAGE GUY THAT'S SEEN HER wants to date her, and millions of young girls all over the world dream of being just like her. She's smart, drop-dead gorgeous, and incredibly talented, which explains why she has become one of the hottest and highest paid young actresses in Hollywood.

Alicia (pronounced "A-lee-see-ah") Silverstone (pronounced exactly like it looks) was born October 4, 1976, in San Francisco, California. Her mom's name is Didi (short for Deirdre) Silverstone, and her dad's name is Monty Silverstone. She also has a brother, David. The final member of Alicia's family is her dog, Sampson, who is a combination rottweiler, pit bull, and Doberman. Unlike what you might expect, acting doesn't run in Alicia's family. Her mother used to be an airline stewardess, and her father is a successful real estate investor.

Back when *Clueless* was first released in theaters and Alicia was interviewed by David Letterman in July 1995, she told him, "When I was three or four, I would dance to Olivia Newton-John on my coffee table. . . . I used to think my mom was Olivia Newton-John. . . . She's a stewardess, so she was always flying. I used to think when she left, she was going to do a concert."

Both of Alicia's parents are from England. While the family now maintains homes near San Francisco and in Los Angeles (Bel Air), as Alicia was growing up, she spent much of the year near San Francisco. The majority of her summers were spent with her family in England.

Alicia has lovely green eyes, brown/blond hair, and is approximately five feet 9 inches tall. Like many actors and actresses, Alicia's first major acting role was in a television commercial. The commercial was for Domino's Pizza, and she appeared in it when she was fourteen. From there, she went on to star in several movies and the

megapopular Aerosmith music videos—
"Crazy," "Amazing," and "Cryin'." MTV has
called the "Cryin'" music video the "Best
Video of All Time," and awarded this honor
at the MTV Music Video Awards. In an
interview with her hometown newspaper,
the *San Mateo Times*, Alicia stated, "MTV is
awesome, and so powerful. They can do so
much for young people and for the world.
I'm happy that MTV likes me."

While it was her roles in the music videos
that captured the attention of her early
fans, Alicia's first role in a major motion
picture was in *The Crush* back in 1993. The
original script for *The Crush* included several nude scenes for Alicia's character. However, Alicia has always refused to do nude
scenes, so the script was changed to accommodate her. In addition, a body double
was used for several of the more revealing
scenes in the film. At the time *The Crush*
was filmed, Alicia was a minor, which put
serious limitations on the number of hours
she could work each day. In order to meet
the film's busy shooting schedule, Alicia
was legally emancipated at the age of fifteen (and also earned her G.E.D.). This
meant that according to California law, she
was considered an adult and could work
adult hours. Being legally emancipated

allowed her to work full-time, starting with her role in *The Crush*.

Because of her stellar performance in *The Crush*, Alicia won two MTV Movie Awards that year—"Best Breakthrough Performance" and "Best Villain." (If you missed seeing *The Crush* in theaters, check it out on video, and you'll immediately understand why she won these awards.)

Thanks to the success of *The Crush*, Alicia was offered many additional acting roles. Some of the roles that she chose *not* to accept (or that she auditioned for but did not get) were the young female leads in the movies *My Father the Hero* and *Little Women*. She turned down the opportunity to replace Shannen Doherty on the Fox Television Network's hit show *Beverly Hills, 90210*. Alicia also chose not to reprise her role as Cher in the television series adaptation of *Clueless* (which premiered in September 1996). Instead, teen actress Rachel Blanchard won the role—but more on that later.

One of Alicia's early acting roles was as a guest star on ABC-TV's *The Wonder Years* during the show's fifth season (episode 80). She played Kevin's dream girl in an episode called "Road Test" that originally aired on November 8, 1992. In this episode, Kevin

(Fred Savage) kept trying to get a date with Alicia's character, but she wasn't interested because Kevin didn't yet have his driver's license. Alicia has told reporters that she used to have a major crush on Fred, and that when she first met him on the set, she turned bright red and was nervous.

A company called Anchor Bay Entertainment sells videocassettes of *The Wonder Years* episodes, and you can purchase the episode that Alicia appeared in by writing to: Anchor Bay Entertainment, Inc., 500 Kirts Blvd., Troy, MI 48084.

By 1993, Alicia was working hard, filming movies back-to-back. In fact, her work schedule has been busier than that of most popular movie actors and actresses for the past few years. Alicia takes little time or no time off in between her movie projects. Some of the films she has starred in, like *The Babysitter* and *TrueCrime*, were never actually released in theaters, but you can now rent them on video or see 'em on cable television.

Despite having acted in many movies prior to her starring role in Paramount Pictures' *Clueless*, it was this blockbuster film that transformed her into a teen superstar. Since the summer of 1995, when *Clueless* was released in theaters, Alicia has become a household name in America and around the world. For her role in *Clueless,* Alicia has won numerous awards, and has been featured in just about every major magazine and on every television talk show you can think of.

Since filming *Clueless,* Alicia has worked on several other films and has cut an awesome three-year (nonexclusive), multipicture deal with Columbia Pictures. Alicia, along with her best friend and manager, Carolyn Kessler, have founded First Kiss Productions, which is based on Columbia Pictures' studio lot in Culver City, California. Through First Kiss Productions, Alicia will both star in and produce motion pictures, starting with the film *Excess Baggage.* Barry Josephson, president of production at Columbia Pictures, negotiated the deal for Alicia to produce and star in movies for his company. After signing the deal, he was quoted as saying, "We're very excited to welcome Alicia to the Columbia Pictures family. We have every confidence in her enormous talent and box office appeal, and are looking forward to working with her on *Excess Baggage* and other future projects."

As the star of the action-comedy *Excess Baggage,* Alicia played opposite Christopher Walken. This film began production in late-winter 1996. Any additional films that Alicia will star in and produce under this Columbia Pictures deal will most likely have to wait a while. After all, she stars as Batgirl in the fourth Warner Bros. Batman movie, *Batman and Robin*, which has one of the biggest all-star casts in Hollywood history. This latest Batman flick began shooting in September 1996. *Batman and Robin* is directed by Joel Schumacher and produced by Tim Burton. Alicia worked with Joel Schumacher when he produced *The Babysitter*, so the well-known producer/director was already familiar with her talents long before work began on the latest Batman movie.

When discussing her career, Alicia says, "It's all happening so fast. Every day it's like, 'What's next?' There's so much excitement. It doesn't feel real." After all, Alicia is living the Hollywood dream. After long days of work, and on the few days off she has, Alicia attends many of Hollywood's biggest events, like the Academy Awards, the MTV Movie Awards, the Genesis Awards, various charity events, and those star-studded movie premieres.

Even though Alicia is considered a superstar in Hollywood, she's a down-to-earth young woman who has wanted to be a serious actress for as long as she can remember. "Ever since I was a little girl, acting was my dream. I always knew I wanted to do what those people on stage did," she's said. In addition to acting in major motion pictures and in television movies, Alicia also has a passion for acting onstage. She appeared in a theatrical production in Los Angeles called Carol's Eve. When she has time, like after she completed filming *Clueless*, Alicia studies acting and takes acting classes at world-famous acting schools like Shakespeare & Company in Lenox, Massachusetts.

Seeing her in movies playing characters like Cher in *Clueless*, you'd probably think that in real life Alicia is extremely confident in herself and her acting abilities. Wrong! She actually considers herself to be something of a klutz and a goofball. She's told reporters from *Teen Beat* magazine, "I'm just some whacked-out, freaky little tomboy. Every time I step into something, I'm convinced that I'm going to fail, and it's really horrible. But it's also what keeps me going." Despite what you might think, Alicia is also not into fashion. In fact, in real life she says she enjoys wearing sweatpants and her favorite T-shirt. She once told *Teen*

*Beat,* "I'm not into clothes. I can't stand wardrobe fittings. They infuriate me because I'm not into that stuff—it makes me dizzy, especially in department stores when you see all those silver racks coming at you. Besides, I hate the way everything looks on me." She told *Entertainment Weekly* magazine, "This is very weird for me, that people would even think of me as being pretty. When I look in the mirror, sometimes it's very sad because I feel like this ugly, fat blimp, you know? And then I have to go be this beautiful girl when I'm in public."

Alicia never truly planned on being a megasuccessful movie star. All she ever really wanted to do was act. When she was around thirteen, she was a member of a San Francisco–based acting troupe that happened to be in Los Angeles to participate in a talent showcase. It was at this showcase that her manager discovered her. Carolyn Kessler, Alicia's friend and manager, has stated that it was Alicia's very genuine quality and soul that jumped out at her. Since Alicia and Carolyn started working together, Alicia's parents have stayed in the background, providing support but not getting involved in the day-to-day business activities relating to Alicia's busy and highly successful career. Alicia now has a manager, an agent, a team of lawyers, and one of Hollywood's top publicists assisting her in managing her career. For their part, her parents offer plenty of love and support.

No matter what their occupation, the truly successful people in the world are those who really love their work. These people don't do what they do for the money, they do it because it's something they love. Some people graduate from college or graduate school and have absolutely no clue what they want to do for a career. Many others start their career, but wind up switching jobs and careers many times until they find an occupation that they enjoy. For the most part, the majority of young people don't get their first after-school or summer job until they're in their late teens, and they don't launch a career until they're in their twenties—but not Alicia! As a child, Alicia knew exactly what she wanted to do with her life, and she's done everything within her power to make her dreams come true. This is one of the many things that make Alicia special. Sure, she's still in her very early twenties, and she could decide to leave show biz altogether sometime down the road, but right now it's her passion for acting, and most recently producing, that has allowed Alicia to be successful in her career. By the time she was fourteen, Alicia had launched a career as an actress: she had a manager and was auditioning for major acting roles. By the age of twenty, Alicia was an actress and a movie producer. What's next, you ask? The only person who knows for sure is Alicia herself.

# two

## Lights! Camera! Alicia!

SOME EXTREMELY TALENTED AND GOOD-LOOKING people dream of becoming famous actors and actresses and work their entire life to achieve that goal. Alicia Silverstone, on the other hand, has worked extremely hard, but has been lucky enough to experience tremendous success at a young age. Her looks and talent have been important ingredients in her success, and have allowed her to work virtually nonstop since 1993, making back-to-back movies.

In case you've missed any of Alicia's major television or motion picture performances, here's a summary of what she's done so far. Her rise to superstardom began with the Aerosmith music videos and her starring role in *The Crush*.

## THE AEROSMITH VIDEOS

Her appearances in three Aerosmith music videos—"Cryin'," "Amazing," and "Crazy"—first gave Alicia worldwide exposure. All three of these videos continue to air often on MTV, and they're also featured on a videocassette called "Big Ones You Can Look At" from Geffen Home Video (suggested retail price $24.95). This videocassette is a compilation of thirteen of Aerosmith's most popular music videos, and also offers some behind-the-scenes footage of the group and the making of the videos.

### *"Cryin'"*

This popular music video was shot in Fall River, Massachusetts, Aerosmith's home turf. The "Big Ones You Can Look At" videocassette features some lost footage that never made it into the music video.

When the actual music portion of the video begins, Alicia is in a movie theater, paying practically no attention to what's happening on the screen, because she's staring at two lovebirds, one of whom appears to be her character's boyfriend, making out a few rows in front of her. Alicia's (soon-to-be-ex)boyfriend in the video is award-winning actor Stephen Dorff. The lyrics of the song describe the singer's bittersweet feelings about finding and losing love. The video wraps up with Alicia jumping off a bridge (apparently to commit suicide) while her boyfriend watches. This stunt is designed to trick him, because she is really hanging from a wire, and winds up bungee-jumping, then giving him the finger.

*"Amazing"*

Yup, she's amazing (but if you're a fan of Alicia's, you already knew that)! This music video was shot in Boston. Like many of Aerosmith's music videos, it was directed by Marty Callner. This video has sort of a high-tech computer twist, and features actor Jeremy London as a computer nerd who finds Alicia's character in cyberspace. The rest of the video is a trip into virtual reality, and shows the fantasies of young computer hackers. Cool computer graphic effects, the music of Aerosmith, and Alicia on a BMW motorcycle . . . what more could anyone want? How about an exciting airborne finale!

*"Crazy"*

For this music video, Aerosmith and Alicia traveled to Hollywood and Santa Barbara, California. This time, Alicia costars with Steven Tyler's daughter, Liv Tyler, who has become a celebrity in her own right.

They're young and innocent private school girls at the beginning of this video, but you'll quickly discover that both Alicia and Liv's characters have a wild side to them. As they escape from their school, the girls shed their uniforms and go cruising in a convertible. The duo drop into a convenience store, smile seductively at the cashier, and walk off with loads of free stuff. Their journey continues as they drive through farmland and pick up a cute young farmer stud who abandons his tractor to go for a swim with the girls in a nearby lake. Is this whole thing real, or just a daydream? Oh, and for a touch of déjà vu, Jeremy

London from the "Amazing" video makes a cameo appearance at the end, playing a hitchhiker.


ALICIA'S EARLY MOVIES

Now, let's jump back to 1993, when Alicia worked on three movies—*Scattered Dreams*, *Judith Krantz's Torch Song*, and *The Crush*. Obviously, it was her starring role in *The Crush* that transformed her from being considered an "Aerosmith video chick" (a term Alicia totally hates) to being thought of as an actress.


*Scattered Dreams*

*Scattered Dreams* was a made-for-television movie that costarred Tyne Daly (from the TV series *Cagney & Lacey*) as "Kathryn Messenger," Gerald McRaney as "George Messenger," Sonny Shroyer as "Sheriff Ashford," and Andrew Prine as a guy called "Sandstrom." It originally aired on December 19, 1993.

In case you missed this television drama,

George and Kathryn Messenger were parents of five children (one of which was Alicia's character, "Phyllis Messenger"). The Messengers were extremely poor, kind, and uneducated people living in the 1950s in rural Florida. Early in the movie, George and Kathryn are arrested and sent to jail for eighteen months on trumped-up fraud charges. When they're released from jail, the parents discover that their five children have become wards of the state, and they must fight to get them back.

*Judith Krantz's Torch Song*

In this made-for-television movie, Alicia once again got to costar with big-name Hollywood stars, including sex symbol Raquel Welch and Jack Scalia. *Torch Song* was written by best-selling author Judith Krantz, who has sold over 75 million copies of her novels, which include *Scruples, Dazzle, Lovers,* and most recently *Spring Collection*—all of which have also been made into television miniseries. *Torch Song* originally aired on May 23, 1993.

*The Crush*

Produced by Morgan Creek, *The Crush* (now available on videocassette) is a psycho-thriller about a young girl who at first seems totally normal, but who becomes extremely jealous and possessive of an older guy that comes to live in her family's guest house. The story begins with a character named Nick Elliot, who is looking for a new place to live. Nick works as a writer, and needs to find somewhere that's quiet and peaceful so that he can work and relax. He discovers that the Forrester family has a guest house that's available for rent, and decides to check it out.

While visiting the Forresters, Nick meets fourteen-year-old Darian Forrester (played by Alicia), who we learn keeps pretty much to herself and has only one friend. Darian quickly develops an obsessive crush on Nick (hence the movie's title). Once Nick moves in, he and Darian spend time together as friends—that is, until Nick meets Amy (a woman his own age whom he begins dating). That's when Darian starts getting extremely jealous, and does just about anything to keep Nick for herself.

If you haven't seen *The Crush*, and you enjoy somewhat scary films, then it's definitely worth renting. The entire film was shot in Vancouver, British Columbia. For her work in *The Crush*, Alicia won the "Best Villain" and "Breakthrough Performance" awards at the 1994 MTV Movie Awards.

### Cool and the Crazy

In 1994, Alicia worked on a film for Showtime in which she portrayed a young woman in her twenties. Michael and Roslyn (Alicia's character) are high school sweethearts who get married and have a child right after graduation. The couple, however, quickly discover that being parents and having to transform from partying high school kids into responsible adults isn't easy. As a result, Michael and Roslyn begin having financial and other problems, and drift apart.

*Cool and the Crazy* isn't Alicia's best work, and the story itself is rather bizarre. Heartthrob Jared Leto (My So-Called Life) portrays Michael, while Jennifer Blanc (Party of Five) plays Joanne. If you want to see how cute an on-screen couple Jared and

Alicia are in drama with elements of a thriller, then check it out when it airs on Showtime. Oh, and if you're thinking about getting married right after your high school graduation, this movie will certainly make you think twice.

1995 WAS ALSO A VERY BUSY YEAR FOR ALICIA

With several movies under her belt, Alicia started getting lots of movie offers. In 1995, she had great roles in five movies, including *Le Nouveau Monde* (*The New World*), *TrueCrime*, *Hideaway*, *The Babysitter*, and of course, *Clueless*. Not even the biggest stars in Hollywood normally work on this many film projects in a single year!

*Le Nouveau Monde (The New World)*

This movie takes place in Orleans, France, in 1959. A group of American GIs are in France. Patrick, a seventeen-year-old French teenager, wants to travel to America and become a citizen. One night, he has an accident. He is found by an American family, who take care of him. Later that night, he meets Will Caberra and Trudy Wadd (Alicia's character). Patrick immediately falls in love with Trudy and becomes friendly with Will. That's when things start getting interesting.

*TrueCrime*

Produced by Trimark Pictures, *TrueCrime* was never released in theaters, but it is now available on videocassette. In this quasi-thriller, Alicia costars with heartthrob Kevin Dillon, and the two have several romantic scenes together.

Alicia's character, Mary Giordano, is a bit of a geek. She is totally fascinated by detective work and solving crimes, and she spends all of her free time reading about criminals and the crimes they have committed. She reads all of the police and detective magazines, as well as crime stories in newspapers. Mary also has many friends on the police department in her town, since her father was a cop who was killed in the line of duty when she was younger.

Near the beginning of the movie, one of Mary's classmates is murdered, and the murderer remains on the loose. Since the police can't seem to solve the case, or even come up with any clues, Mary takes it upon herself to begin her own investigation—but this leads to trouble.

Through her detective work Mary discovers a clue that links her suspect with a traveling carnival that happens to be in town. She also discovers that other young girls have been murdered in towns where this carnival has traveled to, which means that Mary has discovered that the person who killed her classmate is a dangerous serial killer. The problem is, nobody knows who the serial killer actually is.

To keep her out of trouble and out of the police's hair, a cadet named Tony Campbell is assigned to keep a watch on Mary. Mary manages to persuade Tony to assist her in her unofficial and dangerous investigation. As Mary and Tony begin spending a lot of time together, she begins falling in love with him. It is her first crush.

During a surprise visit to Tony's apartment, Mary discovers evidence that Tony may be involved in the murders. Now she must prove her theories without getting killed herself. Could the man Mary has fallen in love with be a serial killer? You'll have to watch this movie for yourself to find out.

If you're expecting to see a movie with an incredible story, you should probably rent one of Hollywood's recent hits. *TrueCrime* isn't award-winning, but if you're a true fan of Alicia's, you'll want to check out her performance as love transforms her from a geeky and unattractive young girl into a beautiful young woman.

*Hideaway*

*Hideaway* was produced by TriStar Pictures (a division of Columbia Pictures) and was never actually released in theaters, but you can rent it on videocassette (Columbia TriStar Home Video). *Hideaway* has also been shown on Showtime.

Following a car accident, a new medical procedure brings "Hatch Harrison" (Jeff Goldblum) back to life after he's been dead for two hours. The problem is, when Hatch is returned to the living, he is mentally connected to a serial killer whose victims are teenage girls. The link between the killer and Hatch strengthens, causing the killer to begin stalking Hatch's sixteen-year-old daughter Regina (played by Alicia). Hatch sees what the killer sees, and must stop him before his wife Lindsey (played by Christine Lahti) and his daughter are killed. Needless to say, *Hideaway* isn't a comedy!

*Hideaway* is based on the novel by Dean Koontz and offers some pretty interesting special effects. One cool thing about this movie is that the young actor who plays the serial killer, Jeremy Sisto, also had a starring role in *Clueless* portraying Elton. (You know, the guy Cher tries to set up with Tai, who winds up leaving Cher alone in a parking lot after the party in the Valley.)

### The Babysitter

From Spelling Entertainment (the folks responsible for *Beverly Hills, 90210*, *Melrose Place*, and *The Love Boat*) comes this movie that's now available on videocassette (but was never released in theaters). This movie can best be described as a very strange thriller, in which Alicia's character, Jennifer, plays a teenage baby-sitter about to experience the scariest night of her life.

Harry and Dolly Tucker are a typical upper-middle-class couple with several children for whom Jennifer is hired to baby-sit. Harry, however, is attracted to Jennifer. Throughout the evening in which this movie takes place, while he gets drunk at a friend's cocktail party, Harry fantasizes about a romantic get-together with Jennifer. Meanwhile, Jennifer's teenage boyfriend, Jack, is spending the evening alone after getting into a fight with her. While sitting in a diner, he meets up with another teenager, Mark, who also has a crush on Jennifer. Mark pretends to be Jack's friend and offers him advice for getting back together with Jennifer, but he has an ulterior motive—to get Jennifer for himself.

During the evening, things get totally out of control, and someone winds up dead. To find out who lives happily ever after and who gets a one-way ticket to the morgue, you'll have to see this bizarre movie for yourself. *The Babysitter* is full of surprises and plot twists that will keep you guessing until the very end. Throughout this movie, you'll have to keep track of what's real and what's happening within the various characters' imaginations.

If nothing else, *The Babysitter* will make you wish you had Alicia as your babysitter when you were younger.

*Clueless*

Paramount Pictures' *Clueless* is, without a doubt, the high point thus far in Alicia's career. It was this movie that catapulted her into superstardom and made her a household name—as if you didn't already know that. Duh.

Alicia received great reviews for her work as Cher, and won several awards, including "Most Desirable Female" and "Best Female Performance" at the 1996 MTV Movie Awards; "Best Actress, Motion Picture" at the 1996 American Comedy Awards; "Best Breakthrough Performance" at the 1996 National Board of Review of Motion Picture Awards; "Best Performance by a Newcomer" at the 1996 *Premiere* Magazine's Reader Poll Awards; and "Best Female Newcomer, Theatrical" at the 1996 Second Annual Blockbuster Entertainment Awards. *Clueless* was also nominated for "Best Film" and Alicia was nominated for "Best Comedic Performance" at the 1996 MTV Movie

Awards, but these awards went to others.
(For more inside scoop on *Clueless*, see
chapter 4.)

### Excess Baggage

The first movie to be produced by Alicia's
own production company, First Kiss Productions, is *Excess Baggage*. This is the first
movie which falls under Alicia's multipicture, $10 million deal with Columbia (Sony)
Pictures. Originally, this film was supposed
to be released in theaters in early 1997, but
it was delayed. Watch for it to be released
in late summer 1997. (For more on *Excess
Baggage*, see chapter 6.)

### Batman and Robin

Next to Cher in *Clueless*, Alicia's portrayal of Batgirl in Warner Bros. *Batman
and Robin* is her biggest role yet. After all,
this movie has one of the hottest casts ever
assembled.

### Breakers

Costarring with Anjelica Huston (best
known to young moviegoers as Morticia

Addams from *The Addams Family* movies),
Alicia will begin work on the comedy
*Breakers* in April 1997. Anjelica and Alicia
portray a mother-and-daughter con team
based in Palm Beach, Florida. United Artists produced this movie.

# *three*

## Don't Be Clueless About *Clueless* . . . (Even if You Are in Fact Clueless)

BEFORE ALICIA WAS CAST IN THE ROLE OF CHER IN Paramount Pictures' *Clueless*, she had appeared in many other movies, television commercials, and music videos, but it was this film that propelled her into the ranks of Hollywood's most popular starlets. Just in case you missed this megahit movie in theaters, didn't see it on cable television, and haven't yet bothered to rent it at your local video store (it's now available from Paramount Home Video), *Clueless* is about a sixteen-year-old high school girl living in Beverly Hills, California.

On the surface, Alicia's character seems totally clueless and shallow, but we quickly learn that not only is she highly intelligent, she's also very strong. We see Cher setting up her teachers on dates; adopting the new girl in school and teaching her how to be popular; volunteering for a charity food drive at her school; and helping her father cope with being a busy lawyer and a single parent. Of course, we also learn all about Cher's personal romantic problems, and see her with all of her stereotypical Beverly Hills friends. Alicia says, "Cher knows she's the most beautiful, most obviously important person in the world—her world—yet she doesn't really know about the rest of the world. She evolves in the film and sees there's more to life than her wardrobe. Cher eventually realizes she's beautiful because of who she is inside, not because of her appearance."

The movie was shot entirely on location. *Clueless* began production back in November 1994. The goal was to produce a comedy that depicted the lives of modern-day teenagers on the big screen. To insure that the movie would be legit, careful attention was paid to wardrobe, music, and the overall attitude of the film.

Mona May, the costume designer for *Clueless*, says that she worked very closely with Amy Heckerling, the film's writer and director. "We considered each character's personality, what they would wear and how they would wear it. Cher is the best dressed. She's very chic—Cher would be someone who goes to Paris twice a year to see the collections and bring back all the new fashions. I wanted the film to reflect the latest trends, so I had to do some predicting prior to the runway shows in Paris. I was able to get some hot fashion tips by calling my friends."

No, this movie is absolutely nothing like Fox-TV's *Beverly Hills, 90210*. *Clueless* is a fun-filled romantic comedy and probably the best teen-oriented flick since *Fast Times at Ridgemont High*. No wonder—the person who directed *Fast Times* was the screenwriter and director of *Clueless*, and the producer, too, is no stranger to making teen-oriented movies.

Director/screenwriter Amy Heckerling has written several hit movies, like *Look Who's Talking* and *Look Who's Talking Too*. As a director, Amy worked on *Fast Times at Ridgemont High*, *Johnny Dangerously*, and *National Lampoon's European Vacation*. Amy is a native of New York City. One of her most recent projects has been adapting

*Clueless* into a weekly half-hour television series for ABC-TV. Amy is the series' executive producer. She also wrote and directed the pilot episode of the series, which premiered in September 1996. (You may be wondering why it was decided to make a television series based on *Clueless* instead of a motion picture sequel. Well, according to Amy, she doesn't like doing sequels.)

Since the film *Clueless* was Amy's brainchild, the actress who would be ultimately selected to play Cher was mainly her decision. While the film's credits state that Marcia S. Ross was responsible for the film's casting, Marcia's office reported that by the time she was hired as the film's casting director, Alicia was already signed up for the role.

Amy says that she had a very specific female protagonist in mind. She chose Alicia for the role after seeing her in one of the Aerosmith music videos. "I was on my treadmill watching MTV and that's when I saw the Aerosmith video. I immediately responded to Alicia, as does everybody. She seemed perfect for the role of Cher. She's sexy and pretty, and on the verge of womanhood, yet there is something very vulnerable and childlike about her. Once I noticed her in the video, I saw her in *The Crush* and was impressed with her acting abilities. The big question in my mind was whether or not she could be funny. The studio wanted to see a screen test with Alicia, so we met and she loved the script for *Clueless*. She did a wonderful job on the screen test. For each character, I was looking for something specific," recalls Amy.

"My own high school experience was totally different from anything in *Clueless* or *Fast Times at Ridgemont High*. I attended the High School of Art and Design in New York City. We didn't have a prom because we were too cool. We only wore black, and we were always busy with our art projects," says Amy. "*Clueless* is a fantasy where people can imagine a world in which everyone is beautiful and everyone has money." To help make this film more believable, Amy spent a considerable amount of time hangin' with kids from Beverly Hills High School, and she read dozens and dozens of teen-oriented magazines.

Rounding out the cast in the movie was a talented group of young people, including Stacey Dash, who stars as Dionne, Cher's best friend. "Cher and Dionne have known each other since they were little girls," explains Stacey. "They'll probably still be best friends when they're old and gray. Their names show that their parents were on the same wavelength." In the movie, Cher makes a comment that both she and Dionne were named after famous singers from the past who now do infomercials. Alicia adds, "Dionne is just as fashionable as Cher. They relate to being totally gorgeous and understand each other's problems, such as when one of them can't find the perfect shoes to match their dress. One difference, however, is that Dionne is involved in a relationship, while Cher doesn't think high school boyfriends are worthwhile."

Actress Brittany Murphy costars with Alicia and Stacey in *Clueless*. Her character, Tai, is the outcast new student whom Cher helps to fit in. Cher gives Tai fashion advice and tries to set her up with popular guys.

Actor Paul Rudd portrays Josh, Cher's stepbrother, who winds up as Cher's boyfriend by the end of the film. Paul describes his character as "a freshman in college who listens to R.E.M., reads Nietzsche, and grows goatees in an attempt to think in a free, enlightened way."

Throughout the movie, we also meet

several of Cher's other friends, like Murray (Dionne's boyfriend), Amber, Elton, and Christian. Here's the scoop on the main cast members from *Clueless:*

STACEY DASH (Dionne) has worked with Penny Marshall in the film *Renaissance Man*. She's also appeared in *Mo' Money, Twist of Fate,* and *Moving*. Stacey was born and raised in the Bronx, New York. Before breaking into movies, she made guest appearances on several popular television series, including *The Cosby Show*. Currently, she's starring on the *Clueless* television series with several of the other movie cast members.

When asked if she thought that the rich kids in Beverly Hills deserved to be made fun of in *Clueless*, Stacey responded, "Yes, because they're so stereotyped. This movie, however, gives them heart and shows that they care. In *Clueless*, I don't think we trashed anyone. We made fun of people who are superficial and who have lots of toys, but we didn't put anyone down. When I was in high school, we certainly had cliques. I remember hanging out with a bunch of Italian and Puerto Rican boys, and we used to go out disco and salsa dancing. When I was preparing for my role in *Clueless,* I had to imagine what I would have been like if I had all of that money. Dionne is cool and confident. I think Amy did a wonderful job creating characters of color and with different sexual preferences. She made each character totally acceptable."

Before Stacey went to work on the *Clueless* television series, which started production in July 1996, she costarred in a movie with David Caruso and Kelly Lynch. In *Cold Around the Heart,* Stacey portrays a runaway. The movie is about a man who is hunting for the woman who set him up to take the fall for a triple murder during a jewelry holdup. *Cold Around the Heart* was executive-produced by Oliver Stone.

JUSTIN WALKER (Christian)—*Clueless* was Justin's first movie role, although he performed on Broadway in Neil Simon's play *Lost in Yonkers.* Justin was born in Honolulu. His father is a naval officer and his mother is a ballet dancer. Growing up, Justin lived in San Diego, Washington, D.C., Los Angeles, San Francisco, and Boston. While living in Boston, he attended Brookline High School, and it was there he started acting. "I remember in my high school in Brookline, Massachusetts, we had the stoners, the Jimi Hendrix worshipers, the Asian mafia, and the jocks. It was all there. I think that *Clueless* makes a statement that cliques exist in all high schools. In the movie, we comment on the superficiality of those cliques. I think this movie could take place in almost any city, but the fact that it happens in Beverly Hills provides more stereotypes to poke fun at. I think when kids who really live in Beverly Hills see *Clueless*, they'll wonder what we're talking about when we make fun of them, but I think the rest of the country perceives the kids from Beverly Hills as being just like what we portray in the movie.

"My favorite scene from *Clueless* is the first party scene, because it really shows what most of the main characters are all about. I am very pleased with how my character is portrayed in the movie. Before I accepted the role, I thought about what drawbacks there might be in portraying a gay character in a movie, but I was given an opportunity to be featured in a major motion picture, and that was a chance I could not refuse. I am honored to be in this movie." When asked to describe Alicia, Justin said, "Alicia exudes sexiness. But it's the fact that she's so unaware of it that makes her so special."

• • • •

PAUL RUDD (Josh)—Paul was born in Passaic, New Jersey, but growing up he moved around a lot because his father worked for a major airline. He attended Shawnee Mission West High School in Kansas City, then attended the University of Kansas, where he majored in theater. You might have caught Paul in the movie *Halloween 4: The Return of Michael Myers,* or on the television series *Sisters* or *Wild Oats.* He also costarred in the television movies *The Fire Next Time, The Anello Family Story,* and *Runaway Daughters.* "I think a lot of people see *Clueless* and expect a mindless comedy. Most people come out of the theater pleasantly surprised. Alicia has presence. You can see there's something behind the eyes. She's so charismatic."

DONALD FAISON (Murray)—Donald's acting debut was in the movie *Juice,* which he followed up with an appearance in *Sugar Hill* and then in the Spike Lee film *New Jersey Drive.* He also costarred in *Waiting to Exhale* (with Whitney Houston). Donald was born and raised in New York City. One of his earliest television appearances was on *Sesame Street.* "My high school was for young people who were in show business, so the actors hung out with the other actors, and the dancers hung out with the dancers. During my first two years of high school, I wasn't that popular. In my junior year, I joined the yearbook committee, and I put my face on every single page of the yearbook. That helped me to get noticed," says Donald. "My favorite scene in *Clueless* was the freeway scene, because at the end of that scene, I got to kiss Stacey Dash [Dionne]. That was my first on-screen kiss." Donald currently stars in the *Clueless* TV series.

BRECKIN MEYER (Travis)—You saw him in the movie *Freddy's Dead: The Final Nightmare*, but it was his real-life high school education that helped him prepare for his role in *Clueless*. While he was born in Minneapolis, Breckin moved to Los Angeles at the age of two, and later attended Beverly Hills High School, although he lived outside the school district. "I was like Andrea from *Beverly Hills, 90210*. I had to lie about my address in order to attend Beverly Hills High School," he says. "I guess by saying this I'm admitting to watching that show."

As a child, Breckin starred in many TV commercials and did voice-over work. He even provided one of the character voices in the animated movie *An American Tail*.

"When I was in high school, I was a dork. I was aware of the presence of cliques, but I wasn't part of them. I hung out with people who were my friends. *Clueless* was a fantastic movie because of Amy Heckerling. She is the coolest. When I first read the script, I thought it was dead-on. The kids had expensive clothing, cellular phones, beepers, and nice cars. My favorite scene in *Clueless* is when Tai and Travis first meet. When we did the scene, we did some ad-libbing." Breckin clearly remembers the first time he met Alicia. "I was expecting the Aerosmith girl to walk in, wink and make me melt, then go off with an entourage. But she is so sweet and real, nothing like the girl in the video."

BRITTANY MURPHY (Tai)—Just before landing her role on *Clueless*, Brittany co-starred with Tia and Tamera Lowry in the Warner Bros. television series *Sister, Sister*. Before that, she costarred in the TV series *Almost Home*, which aired on the Disney Channel. Brittany is from New Jersey, and moved to Los Angeles at the age of thirteen. Some of her other television appearances have been on *Drexell's Class, Frasier, Murphy Brown, Parker Lewis Can't Lose,* and *Blossom in Paris.* Outside of her acting, Brittany is extremely active in several charities, including the Make-A-Wish Foundation, the Starlight Foundation, the Cystic Fibrosis Foundation, and the Easter Seal Society.

"In my own high school experience, kids hung out with people based on their activities and involvement in the school. The time this was most noticeable was at lunch, when people got together in their little groups. In high school, most people try to latch onto a group which becomes part of their identity," says Brittany. "I think one reason why *Clueless* is so popular is because everyone who is in high school, or who went to high school, knows people who were just like Cher and Dionne, and they can relate. My favorite scene in the movie was the freeway scene. I also like the scene when Cher and Josh discover that they love each other."

JEREMY SISTO (Elton)—He was born in Grass Valley, California, but when he was three his family moved to Louisville, Kentucky. Four years later, his family moved to Chicago, where he began acting with a local theater group. You might have seen Jeremy in the movies *Grand Canyon*, *The Crew*, *Moonlight and Valentino*, or *White*

*Squall*. He also starred as a serial killer in the movie *Hideaway*. This was the first time he and Alicia got to work together on a movie, although both actors had very different types of roles than they later did in *Clueless*.

ELISA DONOVAN (Amber)—Originally from Poughkeepsie, New York, Elisa grew up on Long Island. To film *Clueless*, Elisa took time off from college. She credits her late uncle, theater actor Warren Hino, for getting her interested in acting. If you were a fan of the soap opera *Loving*, you might remember seeing Elisa in her role as Jennifer. She also made a guest appearance on NBC-TV's *Blossom* as Joey's girlfriend. Most recently, Elisa has reprised her role of Amber in the TV version of *Clueless*.

Well, those are the young cast members of *Clueless*. Dan Hedaya (who played Mel, Cher's father) has been featured in many popular movies, including: *To Die For, Maverick, Searching for Bobby Fischer, Rookie of the Year, Mr. Wonderful, The Addams Family, Tightrope,* and *Nixon*. Wallace Shawn, too, (Mr. Hall in *Clueless*) has been in a number of movies, such as *Radio Days* and *The Hotel New Hampshire*. Twink Caplan

(Miss Geist in *Clueless*) also worked behind the scenes as the film's associate producer. She has worked with Amy Heckerling for over a decade as a producer and as an actress, and is currently both starring in and working as associate producer on the *Clueless* television series. Julie Brown (Ms. Stoeger) cowrote and appeared in the movie *Earth Girls Are Easy*. She also appeared in several other films, and in the MTV series *Just Say Julie*.

*Clueless* producer Scott Rudin knows what it takes to make a hit movie. In fact, almost every movie he's worked on becomes a box office hit. Some of his recent projects include: *The Firm, Sister Act, The Addams Family, Addams Family Values, Little Man Tate, The Brady Bunch Movie, A Very Brady Sequel, The First Wives Club*, and *Mother*.

From the start, *Clueless* was destined to become a hit. The soundtrack (available on Capitol Records) includes music from: Cracker, Counting Crows, World Party, Luscious Jackson, Radiohead, Coolio, Beastie Boys, Mighty Mighty Bosstones, Jill Sobule, Lightning Seeds, Velocity Girl, Smoking Popes, Supergrass, and The Muffs. The week the film was released in theaters across America, the cast hosted a special premiere beach party that aired on MTV.

## DON'T GO THROUGH LIFE SPEAKING LIKE YOU'RE MENTALLY CHALLENGED!

Okay, so you've got a movie with great acting, a wonderful script, awesome music, hot fashions, and a bit of comedy. To top everything off, the movie had its own lingo. So, if you wanna be a totally clued-in *Clueless* fan, here are some vocabulary terms Paramount Pictures thinks you oughta know:

| THE WORD | THE MEANING |
|---|---|
| "As if!" | To the contrary; No way! |
| "Au di" or "I'm audi." | Good-bye . . . I'm leaving; I'm outta here |
| "Baldwin" | A good-looking guy—a male Betty |
| "Barney" | An unattractive (ugly) guy—not a Baldwin |
| "Betty" | A gorgeous woman; a total babe |
| "Big time" | Totally or very |
| "Buggin'" | Pissed off; irritated; perturbed; flipping out |
| "Clueless" | Lost; stupid; uncool |

| | |
|---|---|
| "Fashion victim" | Someone who doesn't dress fashionably, or who abuses the clothing he or she owns by wearing it incorrectly. Amber in the movie and TV series *Clueless* is the perfect example of a "fashion victim." |
| "Golden" | Righteous; special; a babe |
| "Hang" | Get tight with |
| "Hottie" | A hot-looking girl—a babe |
| "Hurl" | Barf; worship the porcelain god; spew; blow chunks |
| "Hymenally challenged" | A virgin |
| "Majorly" | Very; totally; furiously |
| "Mentally challenged" | Stupid or clueless |
| "Monet" | Looks great from a distance, but is really a total mess up close |
| "Postal" | A state of irrational, psychotic anger and disorientation; wacko or flipped out |
| "Random" | Mediocre or wack |
| "Surfing the crimson wave" | Experiencing women's monthly distress |

| "Tard" | Short for retarded; an insensitive, stupid, or childish person |
| --- | --- |
| "Tscha" | Surely you jest; No sh*t! |
| "Whatever" | Don't bug me; Let's not argue; Whatever you say |
| "Wig" | Become irrational, freak out, or go postal |
| "Wo-man" | Your boyfriend's name for you—what Murray called Dionne in the movie |
| "Zup?" or "Wass up?" | Is anything new? What's up? |

Are you feelin' a bit more clued in yet? Good. And now that you know the characters, you can head to your local toy store and pick up the new *Clueless* dolls from Mattel. They'll be available sometime in 1997. Do you remember that scene in the movie in which Cher and Dionne used their desktop computer to choose their outfits? Mattel New Media is developing a software package that allows you to re-create that scene using your own computer. There's also an official line of other *Clueless*-based products, including original novels, T-shirts, posters, calendars, board games, collectable prepaid calling cards, accessories, and school supplies that you can get your hands on.

If you wanna find out more about the movie, you can check out the official *Clueless* Web site on the Internet (http://www.paramount.com/clueless.html). You can interact directly with Cher, who in the opening page of the Web site explains, "A computer is to life what a credit card is to your wardrobe—the ultimate accessory." From this site, you can download pictures of your favorite actors and actresses from *Clueless*.

AVOID BEING A FASHION VICTIM

*YM* magazine reported that if you want to look like a Hollywood babe, like Alicia, and have that cute, girl-next-door look, you should "curl your lashes before putting on mascara, line inside your lip line, then apply rose lipstick."

If you're buggin' about your looks, check out what the people responsible for how Alicia looked in *Clueless* say about how you too can become a total Betty. Alan "Doc" Friedman was the makeup supervisor for *Clueless*. He was the guy responsible for making sure Alicia's makeup made her look like a hottie in each and every scene. Alan worked with hairstylist Nina Paskowitz, who kept Alicia's hair looking perfect, and also with Mona May, the costume designer for *Clueless*.

ALAN "DOC" FRIEDMAN CHATS ABOUT MAKEUP

"What we do in motion pictures is not just makeup," explains Alan, who creates his cosmetic character by reading the script carefully, communicating with the actress he'll be doing makeup for, and then communicates with the film's director, producer, costume designers, and hairstylists. "A lot goes into actually putting a character like Cher together. It wasn't just a matter of applying makeup to Alicia in order to make her look more attractive. The makeup in *Clueless* was designed to make Alicia look attractive and likable, yet not look overdone. In Alicia's case, she is very pretty to begin with, so not a lot of correctional makeup was necessary. Normally, if an actor or actress has some type of problem, like a strangely shaped face, a lazy eye, or an uneven skin tone, correctional makeup is required. Alicia did not have any unusual problems that needed correcting, so it was just a matter of enhancing her natural looks.

"In each scene, Alicia's makeup changed,

depending on what her character was wearing and what she was supposed to be doing. One of the things I tried to do throughout the film was to keep Alicia's makeup timeless. I didn't try to make any strong statements with the makeup, because I didn't want to guess the trends and have the makeup look outdated. With *Clueless* available on videocassette and on cable television long after the film was released in theaters, I hoped her makeup would not appear dated. Alicia's makeup is both classic and classy, something that will look as if it's in style many years from now.

"My advice to young women when it comes to applying their own makeup is to avoid what's trendy and stick with a look that's classic. Many people look at their high school yearbook picture a year or two after it was taken, and they can't stand how they look, because their makeup and hairstyle were trendy. At the time it was the in look, but a short time later, it can look very outdated."

When *Clueless* began filming, one of the very first things Alan did was to help Alicia develop a personal skin care system. "Like every young woman, Alicia's skin needed special care, so I put her on a regime of cleansing her face, especially after working a full day wearing makeup. The skin care regime that I suggested Alicia follow involved cleansing, toning, and moisturizing every morning and every evening. As most girls make the transition to being young women, they need to begin caring for their skin. People tend to choose a line of makeup products by brand name and use products only from that line. For Alicia, I used various products from different product lines and manufacturers.

"As a makeup artist, I pick and choose the best products to fit the actors' or actresses' personal needs. Everyone has different skin or complexion issues that need to be dealt with and using the makeup and cosmetics that work best for them helps in the long run. For Alicia, I used a cleanser from one product line and a toner from another. I believe what most young women need in terms of a cleanser is something other than soap, that will liquefy makeup and/or cosmetics and remove it without disturbing the acid mantle of the skin. In addition, whatever someone is using as a cleanser has to be easily rinseable with water. Until recently various greasy or oily substances were used to remove makeup, but the problem was that those substances remained on a person's face, creating one problem and scrubbing them off using harsh soap creates another. For a cleanser, stay away from animal-based soap products, because they will dry out the skin. There are many types of cleansers available, and each works best with a different type of skin. I recommend that you visit your local beauty supply or department store and experiment with various products. From my experience, the less expensive products often work just as well as the expensive ones."

The second part of the skin care regime that Alan designed for Alicia involved toning. "Toning is used to bring the acid balance of the face back to neutral and to make sure that all of the cleanser has been rinsed off. Some women who have very dry skin don't need a heavy alcohol-based toner. When choosing a toner, you have to find one that is designed for your skin type, whether it is oily, dry, or normal skin."

Finally, Alan used a moisturizer on Alicia as the final part of her skin care regime. "A moisturizer will seal and hold the moisture content of the skin. I generally pick moisturizers that contain no mineral oil. Mineral oil–free moisturizers are sometimes difficult to find. Kiehl's makes some good ones, available at high-end department stores. Good moisturizers will use plant or seed oils that are very natural, and blend well with human skin. Petroleum-based or oil-based products should be avoided. To determine what your moisturizer is made with, read the list of ingredients that are listed on the packaging. The purpose of a moisturizer is to keep the skin hydrated. These products work best if applied right after a shower or after the skin has been cleansed, because it is already moist. You want to apply a moisturizer that works almost like a sealant to lock the moisture onto your skin to keep it from drying out and protect it from the environment even if one wears no other makeup."

Alan recommends that even young women who don't wear a lot of makeup apply a moisturizer, in order to protect their skin and create a barrier between their skin and the pollution and dirt that's in the air. "If you're going to be outside, a moisturizer with sunscreen added to it will help to protect your skin from the sun's harmful rays," adds Alan.

While working on *Clueless*, Alan recalls that Alicia's cosmetic process took about twenty minutes. "She didn't need any corrective work, but it took time to make sure her skin remained clean and moisturized as we applied and retouched her makeup in between each scene. For Alicia, I always added a bit of under-eye correction or counter shading, which is something that everyone needs when they're going to be filmed or photographed. Alicia's makeup for *Clueless* usually consisted of mascara, lip gloss, and cheek color. The makeup was a bit more elaborate for scenes where Alicia was supposed to look more glamorous for one of the party scenes. To match the wardrobe, most of the makeup we used was in the matted beige and natural brown family. The eye color we used was usually peach, and looked very crisp and clean. Most of the makeup I used for Alicia is available over the counter from beauty supply or department stores. I didn't use any specialized theatrical makeup (which is usually available only to professional makeup artists). So every young woman has the ability to look 'clueless' (just kidding!)."

In just about every interview Alicia does, she usually states that she doesn't like being pampered or being fussed over at wardrobe fittings. Alan, however, remembers, "Alicia and I got along very well. A lot of people in the movie business can be very condescending to young actresses. I treat

everyone I work with the same—if someone treats me well, I treat them well. Alicia
and I hit it off because I didn't kiss up to
her. I treated her like an adult, with hon-
esty, and like a regular person. She picked
up on that. I was there to do my job, to
have fun, and to make each of the actors
and actresses look good and feel good, and
that's exactly what I did.

"Very few people enjoy sitting still and
having other people paint and poke at
them. I work very quickly, and I try to make
the makeup application and removal experience as pleasant and painless as possible.
Alicia is a professional, and she knows that
makeup is one of those things that she has
to endure, because it's part of her job. The
most difficult days were when they shot
several different scenes from different por-
tions of the script, which meant that Alicia
had to put on and then remove her makeup
multiple times. Most movies are shot out
of sequence, and there is no way this can
be avoided. Despite the busy production
schedule, and the need to constantly apply,
touch up, and then remove Alicia's makeup,
I never received any negative attitude from
her."

Each day that *Clueless* was filming, production began somewhere between 5:00

A.M. and 7:00 A.M. Alicia would arrive at work clean-faced (wearing no makeup). After the day's shooting, she would then remove all her makeup, unless she was going out that evening. "When an actor or actress arrives to work in the morning, part of putting together their character involves hair, makeup, and wardrobe," Alan says. "When they're done working for the day, actors or actresses transform back into themselves, and their makeup is removed, their hair is returned to normal, and they change back into their street clothes. We had setups for Alicia to remove her makeup in her personal trailer, in the makeup trailer, and at her home, so she could cleanse, tone, and moisturize conveniently."

Just about everyone knows that Alicia cares a lot about protecting animals. In the early days of shooting *Clueless*, Alicia made it a point to insure that Alan wasn't using any makeup or cosmetic products that were tested on animals. "We had that conversation and understanding early on. Even before she brought that up, I had stopped using products that were tested on animals. Everything I use, to my knowledge, is 'cruelty-free.'"

Alan says that the color tone of the makeup he used on Alicia was always based on the outfit she would be wearing in specific scenes. "Alicia's hairstyle and makeup changed in relation to the wardrobe. Cher wore many different types of outfits, depending if she was hanging out at home, attending school, or participating in some type of social event or party. One of the biggest challenges the hairstylist and I faced during the production of *Clueless* was maintaining continuity." In *Clueless*, Alicia wore over sixty different outfits, and that required Alan and Nina to make sure that with each outfit Alicia's hairstyle and makeup corresponded correctly.

"It's funny—I go from job to job, but I don't always know which movies I think will be good and which ones won't. Some scripts are very funny and we have lots of fun on the set making the film, but when the movie actually comes out, it bombs because nobody else thought it was funny. In the case of *Clueless*, I didn't feel it would necessarily turn into anything special. I considered it to be a small film, and was very surprised by the critical approval that it has achieved. Out of the dozens of movies I've been the makeup supervisor for, *Clueless* is the one on my resume that now gets the most positive reaction. Working on a project like this is very gratifying. Now that I have seen the completed movie, I don't think there is anything I would change from a makeup standpoint. There are a few minor glitches I see in the makeup, but it's not something that anyone but another makeup artist might notice. These glitches happen when another makeup artist handles the makeup retouches for the various cast members on the set and makes some subtle changes, so the makeup doesn't always perfectly match from cut to cut. I think overall, we were right on the money with the makeup work that was done for this movie."

A year and a half after the film was wrapped up, Alan was asked to supervise the makeup for the *Clueless* television series and to help create the overall look for the TV versions of the characters.

To keep up on the latest makeup trends, Alan recommends doing what he does: "I always flip through the various magazines and visit beauty supply stores to keep tabs on all of the latest products being released. European fashion magazines may help get a jump on what to look for next year, but many magazines, like *Glamour*, *Allure*, *Seventeen*, *YM*, *Sassy*, and *Vogue*, can also help you discover what's new. Having a conversation with the person behind the cosmetics counter at a department store can also be very informative, because they know all of the products that will be available in the next few months, which means they have a general idea of what the future trends in makeup will be. So many different things impact what the newest trends will be, so it's hard to predict what will be next."

KEEPING ALICIA'S HAIR LOOKING PERFECT WAS NINA PASKOWITZ'S JOB

In *Clueless*, it was Nina Paskowitz's responsibility to make sure that Alicia's hairstyle matched the makeup and outfit Alicia wore in every scene. Nina explains, "Determining Alicia's look in each scene was a joint effort between myself, Alicia, Mona May [the costume designer], Alan Friedman [the makeup artist], and Amy Heckerling [the director]. A lot of her hairstyles were decided upon last-minute, based on what we thought would work for each scene and how much time we had for hairstyle changes in between scenes. For every single wardrobe change in *Clueless*, Alicia had a different hairstyle. Because we shot out of sequence, sometimes we had to create a hairstyle that worked just minutes before the scene was shot, and sometimes we had several days to create a look, because the wardrobe for a specific scene was already finalized. There were no set rules for choosing Alicia's hairstyles. Because I'm quick on my feet, and Alicia had a lot of really good ideas, we worked as a good team. We didn't do a lot of research to determine what the latest hairstyle trends would be, because we knew that we needed a timeless look. For each of Alicia's looks, we studied the character and the situation the character was experiencing during a scene, and then we developed a hairstyle that worked and that was appropriate for the scene."

Nina stresses that the most important thing anyone can do in order to have great hair is to take good care of it. "It's important to keep your hair clean. That means shampooing it every day, or at least rinsing it every day. Washing your hair is critical for keeping the pollution out of your hair, especially if you're living in or near a city. The second thing that's important for hair care is moisturizing. This is where most people get into trouble, because they use a lot of conditioner in their hair, and then they rinse it out and blow-dry their hair. Blow-drying your hair without protecting it with a moisturizer is a common mistake. There is a new category of hair products which are leave-in moisturizers that will protect your hair from the heat of blow-drying.

"Another common problem people have with their hair is that it's overprocessed. People put too many chemical treatments in their hair too often. People should try to keep their hair as natural as possible. Excessive blow-drying, coloring, curling, and perming will have a long-term negative impact on anyone's hair.

"The most important thing for a young person to remember is that they should like who they are and take good care of themselves. Everything you do on the inside shows on the outside. There's always room for experimenting with your hair and make-up. When you experiment, avoid using harsh chemicals whenever possible, and have fun finding your own look. Don't be afraid of what your own look is, and don't get pressured into thinking that someone else has the answers for you. People should be themselves, whatever that is. There is a lot of pressure for people to look the same. Even if you want to look different, you're supposed to look different in the same way as everyone else in order to fit in. One of the things that is so great about Alicia is that she's a happy person who really enjoys what she does. She's smart and that shows, not only in her look, but in her whole personality."

Nina says that she didn't have to do too much to keep Alicia's hair looking its best. "In the mornings, Alicia would almost always arrive to work with her hair still wet or damp. We would blow-dry it with a combination of several products, many of which came from the Phyto hair care line. Alicia's hair is naturally pretty straight, so we'd blow-dry it in sections and use a big round brush. We didn't use any hair spray so that we could keep it looking totally natural. The biggest trick was getting each hairstyle right the very first time, so we didn't have to rewet it and start from scratch. Alicia takes very good care of her hair, and it was always in excellent condition. Normally, it would take between five and twenty minutes to style Alicia's hair. If we were in a major rush, I'd have one or two other people work with me to dry sections of her hair at the same time. Typically, Alicia came to me first to have her hair done, then she'd get her makeup done and get dressed, then she'd return to me."

As for Alicia's various hairstyles in

*Clueless*, Nina says, "My favorite was when we had Alicia's hair straight down with some type of clip in it. We did a little bit of back-combing at the crown of her head, which gave the hairstyle a little bit of a sixties feeling, but it didn't look overdone. She looked pretty and it was a fun type of look. I also liked it when we put her hair up using a hair ornament and her hair was flopping over like a fan on top of her head. I know Alicia really likes having long hair, and her favorite styles were when she wore it straight down. We had a lot of fun creating all of Alicia's looks, and no matter what we did, she always looked great. I never had to use any hair color or highlights to enhance her look. No matter what I was doing with her hair, I always took the time to get Alicia's input, and at the same time I worked as quickly as possible."

Looking back at the hectic production schedule, one of the worst problems Nina recalls was when they would spend a lot of time getting Alicia's hair, makeup, and wardrobe totally perfect, and then Alicia's dog would get loose and she'd have to go chasing after him. "That happened a couple of times, and we'd have to put her back together very quickly in order to stay on schedule."

Alicia's alma mater, San Mateo High School.

Before the *Clueless* craze: Alicia at the premiere of *Hideaway*.

The first hint of stardom: Alicia at the *Hideaway* screening.

Alicia and her biggest fan: Mom.

Behind every great woman there's...a great woman. Alicia Silverstone and her *Clueless* director, Amy Heckerling.

Alicia pauses to say hi to her fans at the *Clueless* premiere and MTV beach party.

Photo credit: Tammie Arroyo, Celebrity Photo Agency.

Oh my God, is Alicia showing some shoulder?

Photo credit: Scott Downie, Celebrity Photo Agency.

Alicia holds her own with the big girls, Nicole Kidman and Kelly Preston.

Alicia touches up before a scene, possibly with Clinique Raisin Lip Pencil, which was the color most often used for Cher.

Photo credit: Alan Friedman.

Here are four shots of Alicia taken during her make-up sessions for *Clueless*. The many faces of a Betty!

Alicia takes a break from being the Aerosmith girl, Cher, and all-around media darling, to be herself.

Photo credit: Miranda Shen, Celebrity Photo Agency.

Photo credit: Lisa O'Connor, Celebrity Photo Agency.

Sampson and friend pose for the camera.

Alicia and her brother.

Alicia with a new friend at an
animal charity benefit.

Alicia, spending a slow night with the parents.

At the MTV *Clueless* beach party with Sampson.

Alicia makes a photographer's day at the 1996 MTV Movie Awards.

Photo credit: Kevin Winter, Celebrity Photo Agency.

Photo credit: Janet Gough, Celebrity Photo Agency.

Flush with the success of *Clueless* (which was inexplicably overlooked in the nominations), Alicia nevertheless enjoys herself at the 68th Academy Awards.

Photo credit: Tammie Arroyo, Celebrity Photo Agency.

Alicia displays her easy-going charm.

Photo credit: Janet Gough, Celebrity Photo Agency.

Though so far success has been a sure bet for Alicia, she showed up at
the opening of The Hard Rock Cafe in Las Vegas ready to roll the dice.

Photo credit: Miranda Sher, Celebrity Photo Agency.

Alicia enjoys herself at a screening, wearing the standard accessory of fame.

It's not just at the awards shows that you'll find Alicia: here she is doing her part at the OxFaim Hunger Banquet.

Photo credit: Karnbad Michelson.

Photo credit: Kevin Winter, Celebrity Photo Agency.

Alicia in a stunning frock at the MTV Movie Awards.

Alicia: too adorable!

Photo credit: John Paschal, Celebrity Photo Agency.

How can you not smile when you see Alicia?

Alicia's all dressed up with everywhere to go!

WHAT WOULD *CLUELESS* BE WITHOUT THOSE DOPE FASHIONS?

Costume designer Mona May has worked on many films and television shows, making the actors look their best by selecting the most flattering wardrobe for them. Mona was born in India. At the age of seventeen, she moved to West Germany, where she studied art at Freilburg University. She continued her studies in costume design and illustration in France and Italy. In 1982, she entered the Fashion Institute of Los Angeles. When she graduated, she returned to Germany to work as a designer. Since then, Mona has traveled the world and has worked with many of Europe's top fashion designers. She now lives in Los Angeles and works as a costume designer in Hollywood.

"I had worked with Amy Heckerling in the past on a television pilot. We very much liked working together and shared the same taste in style. A few years later, when Amy began working on *Clueless,* she called me up because she thought I would be the perfect person to design the costumes for the movie. For me, this was a very exciting project because I've always wanted to tie together high-fashion and costume design for film. The biggest challenge I had working on the movie was predicting what the current fashion trends would be when the movie would be released over one year later. It's very difficult to predict what will be fashionable among teenagers so far in advance. I relied on what was happening in Europe to help choose the outfits that the characters wore in the movie. I paid careful attention to the runway shows in Europe, not to what the kids were currently wearing at Beverly Hills High School.

"One of my jobs was creating the various looks for Cher. When I got the script from Amy, we discussed who Cher was and what she would be like. We talked about every single detail about the character, and since she was totally into fashion, we created an overall look for her. In my mind, when I was designing the outfits for Alicia, I kept thinking that Cher would be the type of person who was rich enough to travel to Europe twice each year to see the newest fashions firsthand and then take the coolest fashions back home with her to Beverly Hills. To me, Cher is a high-fashion girl who reads the French fashion magazines and is a trendsetter."

After Alicia was hired she met with Mona and began the extremely time-consuming process of costume fittings. "She came in and we started doing fittings. I worked with her body to determine what outfits worked on her, and which ones went well with her hair and complexion. During the costume fittings, Alicia and I discussed many ideas and really defined who the character was. We also chose the color schemes we'd use. To me, Cher's outfits are timeless. Even a few years from now, she will look beautiful and stylish, because the outfits we selected were subtle. For anyone who wants to look stylish and fashionable, it's very important to determine what works the best for you and your body type. For example, you have to pay attention to the size of your waist and the length of your legs, and choose clothing that is flattering on you. Don't just follow the latest fashion trends. If you have big hips, don't wear hip-huggers just because everyone else is wearing them."

A typical costume fitting involved Mona and Alicia's working together for several hours at a time, trying on up to fifty or sixty different articles of clothing and determining which ones worked on her. "My goal was to accentuate her physical beauty by choosing the clothing that looked flattering on Alicia. Often, this was done by trial and error and then having Alicia mix and match articles of clothing with various accessories. We had to come up with over sixty different outfits that Alicia would ultimately wear in the movie."

In addition to being a costume designer, Mona's background includes fashion design, so she used those talents to design and create original fashions that Alicia wore in *Clueless*. "I designed several of the outfits Alicia wore, like the one she wore to the pool party. In other cases, I used clothing from high-fashion designers from France and then incorporated the work of young fashion designers from New York and Los Angeles. I mixed and matched fashions to create a totally fresh look for Cher that people had never seen before. I wanted to create totally new designs and trends that young people would want to emulate later. One of my goals was to create outfits that anyone could re-create by visiting their local clothing stores, department stores, secondhand stores, and boutiques. Instead of buying a four-hundred-dollar designer jacket, someone can go to a secondhand store and pick up an identical item for under forty dollars. As a result, anyone can use their own creativity to design a stylish wardrobe without spending a lot of money. When someone is trying to design their own wardrobe, the trick is to have fun experimenting. Try to develop your own personal style, and don't take any trend too seriously. Discover what fashions, styles, and color schemes look the best on you. To make yourself look hot, it's important that you wear clothing that fits you properly."

Mona says that all of the store-bought outfits that were worn in *Clueless* were custom-tailored to the specific actor or actress who wore them so that they fit perfectly. "A proper fit is important when it comes to looking your best. Developing great outfits takes time, but you have to have fun with it or else it can become very tedious work. People shouldn't be afraid to visit stores in the mall, or rummage through their own closets and then customize their clothing by cutting off sleeves, shortening a blouse or a skirt, or adding appropriate accessories, such as a belt, to create totally new looks."

While designing the outfits for *Clueless*, Mona says, a conscious effort was made to avoid using any black, brown, or gray. "Amy and I decided that using bright colors kept everyone looking happy and fresh. We wanted to create a colorful environment and not use the drabby colors of reality, which is what young people often wear. In a sense, we created our own *Clueless* world of fashion by ignoring some of the common trends and going off in our own directions."

As for creating outfits for Alicia, Mona says, "We never put Alicia in high heels. She was very fashionable, but we never put her in outfits that were too low-cut or too see-through. She was very much a teenager and a wholesome girl. She didn't look like a runway model, nor did she look slutty. Early on, we set very high fashion standards, and then we stuck to those standards without making compromises."

Mona and her assistants would arrive on the set before Alicia and place the outfits she'd be wearing that day in her trailer. "When we were ready to shoot each scene, it didn't take long for Alicia to get dressed, because all of the outfits were preselected and prefitted specifically for her. Before production began, we spent many, many hours over a two-month period doing costume fittings. By the time we were actually shooting each scene, we knew exactly what Alicia would be wearing, and the clothes fit her perfectly. All we had to do each morning was gather together the appropriate accessories for each outfit, like the belts, earrings, shoes, and handbags, and lay them out for Alicia. One of my assistants was always on hand to help Alicia get dressed."

Mona believes that those who want to use accessories to add impact to their outfits will look better by keeping the outfits simple. "A lot of young people tend to overaccessorize. If you have a few pairs of earrings that you really like and that go with everything, stick with wearing those. Save your more extravagant earrings for special occasions, like when you get dressed up for a date. Don't wear too many accessories at the same time. I personally like silver jewelry. It's affordable, it goes with almost everything, and it looks very nice."

Mona says that Alicia normally dresses very casually in real life. "Alicia looked at the hours we spent doing wardrobe fittings as part of preparing to portray her character. Trying on the clothes and getting comfortable wearing them helped her get to know who Cher was, and allowed the character to become a part of her. It's much easier for actors to transform themselves into their character when they're wearing their costumes. All of the clothes Alicia got to wear were very beautiful, and they came from all over the world. I took the time to explain to Alicia about all of the outfits and the types of fabrics used, and that made the fitting process more interesting for her. Overall, it was fun to work with Alicia, teach her about the clothes, and show her what's out there. Alicia was very lovely to work with."

Some of Mona's favorite outfits for Alicia were those pleated skirts and the jackets with the T-shirts under them. "She also wore a lot of adorable sweaters. We made a point to avoid outfits that were too tight-fitting or too low-cut. Those styles didn't work on Alicia."

Looking back at the finished movie, Mona says that she wouldn't change anything about the fashions that each character wore. "For what I had to work with, I am extremely happy with how everyone looked in the movie. It's a lot harder work creating outfits to be worn in a teen-oriented movie than it is to design a wardrobe for a regular movie. Everyone had to look nice, but also look their age. I didn't want to dress anyone up so that they looked trampy, or like they were thirty years old. I enjoyed working with all of the young actors from *Clueless*."

To keep up on the latest fashion trends,

Mona has to work very hard. She attends fashion shows held by all of the major designers, traveling around the world to attend these shows. She spends a lot of time researching who the hip up-and-coming designers are, and reads all of the fashion magazines from Europe. "Europe is always ahead of us when it comes to fashion trends."

For the *Clueless* television series, Mona is following all of the same fashion rules that she used to create the outfits worn in the movie. "I have to create at least twelve original outfits per episode for each female character. We shoot each episode in five days, which doesn't give me a lot of time. The fashions in *Clueless* are timeless. My goal is to stay at least one step ahead of the current trends and offer designs that are fresh—that people haven't yet seen in the stores."

# four

## Alicia Talks About *Clueless* and More . . .

A FEW WEEKS BEFORE PARAMOUNT PICTURES RE-leased *Clueless* in the summer of 1995, most of the cast gathered at the Four Seasons hotel in Beverly Hills, California, for what the movie industry calls a press junket. At these events, dozens of reporters from across America gather to meet the stars of an upcoming movie. Here's your chance to find out exactly what Alicia told reporters at the press junket for *Clueless*!

*You were born in San Francisco, but you grew up spending summers in London. What was that like?*

ALICIA: "My mom and dad are both English. My brother and I are the first Americans in the family. My mother, Didi, used to be a stewardess for PanAm airlines, so we spent a lot of time in London and America. I have the fondest memories of England. I wish I could go there more often. It was wonderful to experience life in other countries while I was growing up, because it helped me to prepare for my career."

*Growing up, were you popular in school?*

ALICIA: "There were times that I was popular, but there were also times in junior high school in particular that I was a total outcast. I went to Crocker Middle School, located outside of San Francisco, and then to San Mateo High School. My year in high school was great, but, with my acting, it got too hard to have a normal life. I missed it at first, but I love what I'm doing. . . . Growing up, I sometimes found myself around girls who were materialistic and shallow. They frightened me, because I didn't want to become that way."

*Is it true that you take acting classes?*

ALICIA: "Yes. After filming *Clueless*, I spent several weeks attending school at Shakespeare and Company in Massachusetts. I am really eager to learn. From these classes, I learned a lot about language. Looking back, I now realize what an amazing job Amy Heckerling [the writer and director of *Clueless*] did on the script. Four hundred years ago, Shakespeare created words that are no longer used. In *Clueless*, Amy has created new types of descriptive words. I would love to someday act in a Shakespeare production onstage. In the past, I have acted in a play called *Carol's Eve* at the Los Angeles Met Theater. I love doing theater, and I look forward to doing much more of it."

*How do you feel about starring in* Clueless?

ALICIA: "I am very excited about *Clueless*. It's the perfect movie for teenagers. There aren't enough movies that are light, happy, and warm. A lot of people want to have a good time when they go to see a movie, and *Clueless* is the perfect film for that. I am so glad that I've had the opportunity to star in a comedy. Every character I have ever portrayed has been very different."

*How would you describe your character in* Clueless?

ALICIA: "Cher has a huge imagination. She has great potential to be very worldly, but early in the movie, her concerns are limited to her clothing and her makeup. At the end of the movie, Cher finally realizes that it's her heart that's important, not her outward appearance. I look for exciting characters and interesting directors, and most importantly a good script, when choosing my roles. Alicia is so different from Cher, so different. I usually feel really gross, ugly, and disgusting, and I don't think looks are important. It's really important to me what's on the inside. You can't fool me with your outward appearance. I wish people would stop being so concerned about what they look like because society stresses the importance of appearance. It's not important at the end of the day. I believe that what's important is what you are on the inside. That's how I am different from Cher."

*When you were attending high school in real life, were there any girls in your class that reminded you of Cher?*

ALICIA: "There were definitely girls that I did not respect because they were so materialistic. When I was very young, my mother taught me my principles, so girls that were shallow and materialistic always discouraged me. When I was reading the script for *Clueless*, at first I didn't want to play Cher because I thought she was totally shallow, but as I continued reading, I learned that the character has a real love, sweetness, and great confidence. Most importantly, Cher was happy. I don't know too many teenage girls that are truly happy. Cher is also really smart. Some of the things that come out of her mouth are very intelligent, even if she doesn't necessarily understand what she's saying all of the time. She'll say a word that she doesn't know the meaning of, but she'll say it with such complete confidence that you think she knows what she's talking about. One of the things I like most about the character is her relationship with her father. In the movie, you see this girl who you don't think cares about anything but what she looks like, and then you see how much she cares about her father and wants to take care of him because her mother died. Cher is a well-balanced character."

*In* Clueless, *Cher is always dressed in the hippest fashions. In real life, how would you describe how you dress?*

ALICIA: "That was very hard for me. In the movie, I wear something like sixty different outfits, and that required many wardrobe fittings. In real life, I am a sweatpants and sweatshirt girl. That's what I wear when I want to be comfortable. The thing with Cher was that she always wore fashionable accessories with her outfits. These accessories were perfect for Cher, but I personally felt very uncomfortable wearing them. I wound up keeping some of the suits, but I didn't keep any of the accessories that I wore in the movie. My favorite outfits in the movie were those pinstriped suits and the plaid coat that I wore."

*As you read the* Clueless *script for the first time, did it surprise you that Cher was a virgin?*

ALICIA: "I thought that was great! The movie is very funny, but when it's over, you'll realize that you've had this bang over the head about how bad drugs and sex can be for you. In the movie, nobody says,

'Don't have sex.' If any of the characters said that in the movie, it would have actually encouraged people to do it. In the movie, Cher knows that she wants to wait for someone special, but because she's fifteen, she's confused and doesn't know when that's going to be, or what that really means. She just knows that she should be saving herself for someone special, and I think that's an important lesson that everyone should take from the movie. Cher is young and doesn't have a real sophisticated view on sex. People think she knows what she's talking about when it comes to sex and relationships, but she doesn't. As an actress, I never tried to be sexy when portraying Cher in this film. If you're a young girl seeing *Clueless*, you're going to learn a lot from this film, but you're also going to laugh a lot."

*What did you do to prepare for* Clueless? *Did you hang out with any kids from Beverly Hills?*

ALICIA: "No, I didn't. Amy Heckerling spent a lot of time with young people as she was writing the script. My biggest thing for this film was finding a voice. In all of the movies I had done before *Clueless*, my characters were always soft-spoken. Even in *The Crush*, the character I played was totally out there, but she was also very intense and quiet. Cher had to be loud and have this incredible voice. I usually learn my lines on the set while filming a movie, but for *Clueless*, I had to spend a lot of extra time learning my lines because the words Cher uses weren't in my own vocabulary. The biggest thing I had to do to prepare for this movie was to spend a lot of time going over each of my lines over and over again, so that they meant something to me. I don't use phrases like 'as if' or 'whatever,' but when I was playing Cher, I had to make it sound like that was how I normally spoke."

*Growing up, did you watch a lot of high school–related movies, like* Fast Times at Ridgemont High?

ALICIA:   "I didn't watch a lot of movies growing up. I loved *Fast Times at Ridgemont High, Girls Just Want to Have Fun,* and *Sixteen Candles,* but I saw those films recently on video. Most of the films I've seen in my lifetime I have seen within the past few years."

*What was it like learning all of those new words used in* Clueless?

ALICIA: "Four hundred years ago, words were wonderful, so juicy and descriptive. I know I have a lazy tongue; most of the world does. We've lost a lot of vocabulary. In this film, there are words you can really have fun saying."

*In* Clueless *and also in the Aerosmith videos, you portray very sexy characters. Were you looking specifically for sexy roles?*

ALICIA: "I don't think I've ever had a 'sexpot' role, nor have I ever gone out for that type of role. 'Cryin'' and other Aerosmith videos were a great experience, but I don't think I'm ever being sexy in them. I portray a girl that everyone relates to. I don't think of myself as a sex symbol. I have just as many young girl fans as I have male fans." (Alicia also told Hollywood OnLine, "I don't feel like a dreamgirl. I think it's really nice that people see me that way, and a part of me wishes that I got that sort of attention in real life, but I don't. It's just in the movies. I know that what's important is on my inside, and the people that I love know me for who I am, and that's what makes a beautiful relationship. I'm flattered that people think I'm pretty, but in my life, I'm not aware of it. I'm just a weird, dorky girl that hangs out with her dog.")

*When dealing with Amy Heckerling as the writer and your director, did you ever suggest changing any of the lines because you didn't think that's how a teenage girl would speak or react to something?*

ALICIA:   "I've done that with other directors in other films that I've done, but I never did anything like that when working with Amy on *Clueless*. I think Amy is a big kid who is very intelligent. In a way, I think she is Cher. I was very scared after I read the script for *Clueless*, because I kept thinking that I was going to mess up the great lines that Amy wrote. I think *Clueless* was brilliantly written. A lot of adult screenwriters have teenage characters in their scripts but they misjudge the intelligence of real-life teenagers. They believe that teenagers don't have anything important to say. I don't think that's the case at all. From *Clueless*, I think adults will develop a new appreciation for young people and what they have to say."

*How has your acting career interfered with your life as a teenager?*

ALICIA: "Because I've been a working actress, I've never really had a normal teenage life. I don't, however, think I've been deprived of anything. I think everything in my life so far has happened the way it was supposed to happen. I try to imagine what my life would have been like if I had stayed in school and put off my career, and I think I would have gone crazy. When I was fifteen, I took my G.E.D. so that I could star in *The Crush*. As a teenager, at times it got really lonely working mainly with adults. In a period of two years, I did nine movies, so there was no time to play. I used to tell my manager Carolyn all the time that I didn't have any friends my own age, but I soon realized that Carolyn is the best friend in the world. I am very happy with the decisions I've made in terms of pursuing my career. I don't, however, enjoy being in the public eye, but I understand that it's something that goes hand in hand with acting."

*What actor or actress would you most like to meet and have a discussion with?*

ALICIA: "I would love to sit down and have an in-depth discussion with Jodie Foster and hear about everything she's gone through. I had a chance to meet her once at the MTV Movie Awards, but we didn't have a real conversation. For me, everything in my career has happened so fast, there hasn't been a lot of time for me to sit back and plan where things are going."

*Having starred in several Aerosmith music videos, are you a fan of their music?*

ALICIA: "Definitely. I love Aerosmith, but I also listen to performers like Sinead O'Connor, David Bowie, and David Gray."

As a result of the incredible popularity of *Clueless,* Alicia wound up making appearances on many of the top television talk shows and being featured in dozens of national magazines. Here are some of the interesting things that she revealed about herself during the interviews.

When asked about acting, she told a foreign entertainment journalist, "To me what an actor is, is somebody who is just dealing with life. I was a really perceptive little girl, so I really understood what people were thinking and feeling when I met them. I think that really shocked people because I was so young. I found an outlet for all that reality. That's what I think acting is—dissecting the human brain and the human heart and getting it all out."

As for her religious upbringing, Alicia is Jewish and says she grew up in a traditional Jewish home. "I had, and loved, my bat mitzvah. My service was three hours long. It happened to fall on May sixth. I ended up with this long Torah portion so the ceremony ended up being better than the party. . . . My dad likes to keep certain holidays and services and he tries to do the candles every Friday night. I used to feel very religious when I was growing up. I went to temple like four or five times a week. Now, I tend to go to temple about three or four times a year, mainly in San Francisco, because that's where I grew up. I love to go and sing the hymns and all that, but I feel my religion in life is just knowing who you are. That's my definition of religion—knowing who you are, and who you believe in, and just going with that."

Everyone at some point in their life dreams of becoming famous. However, people who actually do become famous often discover that it's not quite all it's cracked up to be. Alicia considers herself an actress, and loves being one. As a result of her acting, she has become one of the hottest young stars in Hollywood, but that's not something she's totally comfortable with. In an interview with Hollywood OnLine, she said, "I feel really judged, but I think everyone is judged throughout their life. Even if I don't feel good one day, someone is going to say, 'You look great, you're beautiful.' Even if I don't feel that way at the time." When you're in the public eye, she adds, "It's almost like people don't let you be who you are and feel what you feel. You're supposed to feel what they want you to feel, and be how they want you to be. That's very hard. I'm just an actress."

# five

## Alicia Visits Gotham City

It was May 1939 when comic book artist Bob Kane created the Batman character and introduced him in the *Detective* comic book #27. Since then, artists, novelists, writers, animators, television producers, and moviemakers have all created new and exciting adventures for the Caped Crusader. With the release of Warner Bros.' *Batman and Robin* in 1997, Bob Kane continues to play an active role, working with DC Comics to oversee the various Batman projects that are currently being produced, including the popular movie series.

In this third *Batman* movie sequel, Alicia costars with the biggest stars in show biz, like George Clooney ("Batman"), Chris O'Donnell ("Robin"), Arnold Schwarzenegger ("Mr. Freeze"), and Uma Thurman ("Poison Ivy"). Joel Schumacher, the director of 1995's highest-grossing motion picture, *Batman Forever*, returns as director of *Batman and Robin*. Other behind-the-scenes talent who returned to work on this latest sequel include: Peter Macgregor-Scott (producer), Akiva Goldsman (screenwriter), Benjamin Melniker (executive producer), and Michael E. Uslan (executive producer). Joel Schumacher and Akiva Goldsman have worked together on four other movies—*A Time to Kill*, *Batman Forever*, *The Client*, and *Silent Fall*.

Most people know George Clooney as one of the doctors on NBC-TV's hit series *ER*, for which he has received several Emmy, Golden Globe, and SAG nominations. George made his motion picture debut in *From Dusk Till Dawn*. Just before starting work on this latest Batman flick, he worked on a film called *The Peacemaker*, and also costarred with Michelle Pfeiffer in a romantic comedy called *One Fine Day*. Despite having a hot movie career, George will remain one of the stars of *ER*, at least for the 1996-97 television season. Since *ER* is produced at Warner Bros. Studios in

Burbank, California, which is where much of the filming for *Batman and Robin* was done, all it took was a series of quick costume changes and short walks between sets for George to film both *ER* and *Batman and Robin* at the same time.

Chris O'Donnell is reprising his role as "Robin" after appearing in *Batman Forever.* Most recently, Chris costarred in the motion picture adaptation of John Grisham's bestselling novel *The Chamber* and with Sandra Bullock in the biographical romance *In Love and War,* a film depicting the life of Ernest Hemingway. You can also catch Chris is many other movies, like *The Three Musketeers, Scent of a Woman, Circle of Friends, Mad Love, Men Don't Leave,* and *Fried Green Tomatoes* (all of which are now available on videocassette).

If you're not familiar with Arnold Schwarzenegger's work, then you've probably been living on some distant planet for the past decade or so. You've seen him in *Twins, Junior, Kindergarten Cop, Total Recall, The Terminator, Terminator 2: Judgment Day, Last Action Hero, True Lies, Commando, The Running Man, Raw Deal, Predator, Eraser,* and *Jingle All the Way,* to name a few of his movie projects. Arnold is also one of the owners of the Planet Hollywood restaurant chain, so chances are you'll be able to see some of the actual costumes and props from *Batman and Robin* at the various Planet Hollywood restaurants. For his role in *Batman and Robin*, it's reported that Arnold earned over $25 million dollars for six weeks' worth of work, in addition to getting a cut of the movie's merchandising profits. Arnold portrays Victor Fries and Mr. Freeze in this latest Batman flick.

Uma Thurman (Poison Ivy) has also had an incredibly busy movie career, starring in one hit film after another. You can catch her in *Pulp Fiction, The Truth About Cats and Dogs, Beautiful Girls, Dangerous Liaisons, Final Analysis, Mad Dog and Glory,* and *Jennifer 8,* all of which are now available on videocassette.

One of the final people added to the *Batman and Robin* cast, joining it just weeks before production began, was Australian-born supermodel Elle Macpherson, who portrays Bruce Wayne's girlfriend, Julie Madison, in the movie. Rounding out this star-studded cast are Michael Gough ("Alfred Pennyworth"), John Glover ("Dr. Jason Woodrue"), Pat Hingle ("Commissioner James Gordon"), Coolio ("Banker"), Vivica Fox ("Ms. B. Haven"), supermodel Vendela Kirsebom ("Mrs. Freeze"), and Jeep Swenson ("Bane"). Rock star Mick Jagger also makes an appearance in the film.

Each time Warner Bros. produces a new Batman movie, the look of the title character evolves. One obvious reason for Batman's different look is that different actors have been featured in the role. Thus far, we've seen Michael Keaton, Val Kilmer, and now George Clooney portray Batman. Each actor has given the character a slightly different look and attitude. Director Joel Schumacher has worked closely with costume designers Bob Ringwood and Ingrid Ferrin to redesign the famous Batsuit for each movie. In this latest movie, the Batgirl suit, worn by Alicia, also had to be created by Bob and Ingrid.

To create each costume worn by Batman, Robin, and now Batgirl, it takes several months of work by a team of designers, costumers, sculptors, foamers, molders, and even "Batsuit Wranglers" (the folks who work on the set to take care of the expensive costumes). For the movie, over forty different costumes are created for each character, using all sorts of materials, such as foam, rubber, and plastic. The formula and exact materials used to create the Batman, Robin, and Batgirl costumes are carefully guarded secrets known only to a few people who worked on the movie.

THE HISTORY OF BATGIRL

Here's a trivia question: What do actresses Yvonne Craig, Melissa Gilbert, and Alicia Silverstone have in common? The Answer: They're the three actresses who have had the honor of bringing the Batgirl character to life on television and motion picture screens.

Yvonne Craig made her movie acting debut in 1959 in *The Young Land*, a Western in which she costarred with Patrick Wayne (John Wayne's son). Later in her career, Yvonne worked with many of the most famous actors and actresses of her time, like Bing Crosby and Elvis Presley. She also had guest-starring roles in some of the hottest TV series in the 1960s and 1970s, including the original *Star Trek*, *The Man from U.N.C.L.E.*, *Land of the Giants*, *Voyage to the Bottom of the Sea*, *My Favorite Martian*, *My Three Sons*, and *The Mod Squad*, as well as the ABC-TV series *Batman*. Despite having starred in over eighteen movies and dozens of TV shows, Yvonne is most remembered as the original Batgirl on television.

Holy clock ticking, Batman, it's been

over thirty years, but the *Batman* television series continues to be extremely popular today. You can catch reruns of *Batman* (which starred Adam West as Batman and Burt Ward as Robin) every day on the fX Cable Network. Yvonne, as Batgirl, appeared in several episodes of the *Batman* television series.

The Batgirl character was created in 1966, and made her debut in *Detective* comic book #359 in January 1967. Batgirl's alter ego is Barbara Gordon, daughter of Police Commissioner James Gordon, and originally a librarian who attends a masquerade ball dressed as Batman. On her way to the party, she saves Bruce Wayne from an attack by the Killer Moth. The quiet and mild-mannered librarian loves the thrill and excitement of being a hero, so she decides to become "Batgirl," Gotham City's newest crime fighter.

When Batgirl was introduced in the comic books, the character wasn't too popular—that is, until Yvonne Craig first appeared on the *Batman* television series as Batgirl. In 1992, *Batman: The Animated Series* brought back the Batgirl character. This time, Barbara Gordon was a college student attending Gotham State University. Melissa Gilbert (you know her as "Laura Ingalls" from *Little House on the Prairie*) provides the voice of Barbara Gordon and Batgirl. In this series, when Batgirl is introduced, she is an annoyance to Batman and Robin, and seems to always get in their way but eventually she joins the Dynamic Duo as a partner. Since Robin and Batgirl are close in age, the two characters develop a flirtatious relationship, which has been carried over into the *Batman and Robin* motion picture, allowing Chris O'Donnell and Alicia to work together and share some "moments" on-screen. It is the animated version of Batgirl that has had the most impact on Joel Schumacher and that gave him the idea to introduce the character into the series of live-action movies. Episodes of *Batman: The Animated Series* are currently available on videocassette.

## GOTHAM CITY IS CREATED IN BURBANK, CALIFORNIA

Located in Burbank, California, on 110 acres of land is Warner Bros. Studios. Since these studios were founded in 1929, thousands of popular movies, television shows, and TV commercials have been filmed here, including *Batman Forever, Batman Returns*, and now *Batman and Robin*.

Warner Bros. Studios is made up of thirty-four soundstages and dozens of exterior sets which re-create locations from around the world. For example, the outdoor Hennessey Street set was created for the movie *Annie*. This re-creation of a New York City street looks totally real; however, all of the buildings are fake. The outdoor set was re-dressed (using paint and other scenery) to look like parts of Gotham City and has been used in all of the Batman movies.

A soundstage is a large building, between 6,400 and 31,300 square feet, which is basically hollow inside. The buildings are between 63 and 98 feet tall, so life-size buildings can be built inside the soundstages and used as sets. Using lighting and other special effects, movies and TV shows can be shot anytime during the day or night. If a movie were to be shot on location, the crew would have to rely on perfect weather, plus only shoot daytime scenes during the day and nighttime scenes at night. With sets built inside soundstages, the lighting (and even the weather) can be totally controlled. If the scene calls for rain, for example, sprinklers are used to create fake rain inside the soundstages. For snow and ice, other types of special effects and set dressings are used, like cotton and small pieces of chopped-up white plastic. These not-so-cold items look like snowflakes on screen.

Within these soundproof soundstages, realistic sets are built, allowing movies and televisions shows to be filmed. Since *Batman and Robin* was considered by studio executives to be a guaranteed hit, a huge portion of the studio's resources was put behind the film.

About four months before production of *Batman and Robin* began, hundreds of people began working seven days a week to build the incredibly elaborate sets which were used in the movie. The majority of these sets were built within soundstages. A typical television show uses only one soundstage, while a motion picture might use two or three. *Batman and Robin,* however, used nine different soundstages for production, plus shot scenes on location in numerous places, including the Los Angeles River (where a motorcycle scene was shot) and Long Beach, California.

Stage 16 at Warner Bros. Studios is one of the largest and most versatile soundstages in the world. It was on this stage that several scenes from *Batman and Robin* were filmed. The entire floor of this 98-foot-tall soundstage can be removed to reveal an underwater tank that's 192 feet by

113 feet, and 4 feet deep. A smaller section in the center drops down another 12 feet. On this soundstage, sets can be created around water and underwater scenes can be shot in a controlled environment.

Virtually all of Gotham City, along with many of the locations where *Batman and Robin* was filmed, was built inside of soundstages. Using wood, plastic, plaster, and a lot of paint, life-size sets were built to look like the buildings you see in the comic books. While careful attention was given to every detail so that each set looked totally real, virtually nothing that you see in the movie actually is. Special lighting and all sorts of special effects were used throughout the movie to create elaborate illusions. In conjunction with scenes featuring Mr. Freeze, to create some of the ice, snow, and smoke effects, large tanks of nitrogen and other chemicals were brought to the soundstage and used in conjunction with paint and other forms of "movie magic." Few expenses were spared when it came to producing state-of-the-art special effects for *Batman and Robin*.

Multiple camera crews were used throughout the production of *Batman and Robin*, so at times several scenes were filmed simultaneously. The entire movie was shot in about a hundred days, and some of that shooting was done at night or on weekends to accommodate the actors' schedules.

If you happened to visit Warner Bros. Studios while *Batman and Robin* was in production, you could walk around the studio lot and peek inside the soundstage doors (when there was no filming going on) and see sets on the nine soundstages being built and painted. Throughout the day and late into the night, preproduction work was virtually always under way, and hundreds of people were always at work building, painting, and preparing for upcoming scenes.

Immediately after a scene was completed, the set was often dismantled to make room for new sets. Just outside each soundstage were large trailers (customized mobile homes) that the stars of the movie used as dressing rooms and places to relax between scenes. There's always a lot of downtime when actors are required to be on the set but no filming is actually being done. Since shooting a single scene in a movie like *Batman and Robin* can take hours, and often days, the actors used their trailers as places to hang out, study their lines, take a nap, or change costumes. The film's costume department, hairstylists, and makeup artists also had their own trailers so that they could get their work done right on or near the set.

In addition to the large production crew and cast, one thing that was in abundance on the set of *Batman and Robin* was security. In addition to the regular studio security guards, Warner Bros. hired additional security to guard the sets, soundstages, and actors. In fact, secrecy around this movie was so tight that anyone caught on or near a set without a photo ID was thrown off the studio lot, and sometimes arrested. The producers of the movie didn't want the media disclosing the plot of the movie or releasing photos of any cast members in costume. How cast members like Alicia appeared in their costumes was supposed to remain a mystery until the movie was released in theaters.

During production in October 1996, a camera crew reportedly working for the television show *Inside Edition* was arrested for allegedly illegally videotaping the production of *Batman and Robin*. The crew was charged with burglary, trespassing, receiving stolen property, forgery of government documents, forgery of driver's licenses, theft of trade secrets, and copyright infringement.

On October 15, 1996, *Inside Edition* aired some behind-the-scenes videotape that was shot on two *Batman and Robin* sets. This video footage was shot on September 13 in Long Beach, California, and showed George Clooney, Elle Macpherson, and Uma Thurman. A second segment aired on *Inside Edition* on October 24. This time, the *Inside Edition* crew got past the heavy Warner Bros. security and shot footage on the studio's Stage 12. George Clooney, Chris O'Donnell, and Uma Thurman were featured in the segment.

In order to catch the camera crew, Warner Bros. staged a sting operation that involved Arnold Schwarzenegger. Since the *Batman and Robin* producers were sure that this unwanted camera crew would return when Arnold began filming his scenes as Mr. Freeze, the Warner Bros. security team was ready. Both uniformed and undercover security officers were used to capture the camera crew when they did, in fact, return to the studio in an attempt to capture Arnold on video for *Inside Edition*. When one of the crew was captured, he had a still camera hidden in his sock. He had taken thirty-five unauthorized pictures on the set. Several videotapes were also recovered by Warner Bros. security and the Burbank Police Department.

Robert G. Friendman, who's in charge of worldwide advertising and publicity for Warner Bros., released a statement just after the *Inside Edition* crew was arrested. He said, "This kind of incident is theft of intellectual property and is a serious offense against the hundreds of people and millions of dollars invested in a motion picture of this scope. The quick detection by *Batman and Robin* producer Peter Macgregor-Scott, as well as our outstanding security and legal responses to this incident, were key in finding the alleged perpetrator as quickly as we did, and we are very grateful to all of them. This trend toward violating the boundaries of journalism and human decency in the effort to get video footage has really become out of control, and I hope responses such as ours will help stop it soon."

One reason you heard so little about the production of *Batman and Robin* was because *all* the media—newspapers, magazines, radio and TV reporters—were kept far away from the sets and the actors during production of the movie. This was, however, the first time in recent history that a member of the media was arrested for attempting to obtain information about a movie.

Meanwhile, as production continued during the fall and winter of 1996-97 on *Batman and Robin*, plans were under way to begin production of the next movie in the series immediately upon completion of *Batman and Robin*. Thus, the same sets and some of the same actors could be used in the next movie, and the next movie could be released more quickly.

The original *Batman* movie was released in theaters in 1989. It wasn't until 1992, almost three years later, that *Batman Returns* hit the theaters. *Batman Forever* followed in 1995 (again, almost three years later). By filming *Batman and Robin* and the fifth Batman movie back-to-back, the producers didn't have to worry about the availability of the actors, plus the studio could save money, since the very expensive sets and costumes would not have to be rebuilt. While *Batman and Robin* was still in production, Warner Bros. wouldn't disclose who would be featured in the fifth Batman flick, but George Clooney, Chris O'Donnell, and most likely Alicia will reprise their roles.

A *BATMAN AND ROBIN* STAND-IN SPEAKS OUT!

For hundreds of professional stand-ins, working on this latest Batman movie was a dream come true. After all, who would pass up an opportunity to work with an all-star cast and some of Hollywood's best-known behind-the-scenes talent in a big-budget motion picture?

In show biz, a stand-in is an actor who works on a television show or movie but isn't actually seen. Stand-ins work with the technical crew and the director to plan camera shots and lighting when the real actors are not on the set. Each main character in *Batman and Robin* had at least one stand-in, plus many of the key stunt people working on the film also had stand-ins.

For one 30-year-old guy whose goal is to become an actor, working for four days as a stand-in on *Batman and Robin* was an exciting experience.

"On the days I worked on *Batman and Robin*, my call-time was 7:00 A.M. After arriving at Warner Bros. Studios, I was told to go directly to Wardrobe. From there, I was sent to the set and I waited for the director to call for the 'second team.' Anytime you work on a movie, there's a lot of waiting, because so many things have to happen before the camera actually starts rolling. During each of the filming days, we had to stand around a lot. Our days on the set were very long, but it was fun to be a part of the production.

"I worked on a ballroom scene, so everyone on the set was wearing a formal suit or gown. Batman, Robin, Iceman, and a handful of thugs and cops were all in the scene. Stunt people had to fly through the air and crash through windows. There are tons of punches and kicks that had to be choreographed. It was very exciting to be there watching how the scene came together. When someone actually sees the movie, the scene I worked on will be relatively short, but it took us several days to film it.

"The whole atmosphere on the set was pretty up-beat, but very secretive. Many of the extras and stand-ins who worked on the movie for long periods of time had to sign special contracts saying that they wouldn't talk about the movie. One thing that I know Alicia's fans will like about *Batman and Robin* is that Batgirl and Robin develop a bit of a relationship, so you'll get to see a bit of romance between the two characters. Movie-goers are definitely going to get their money's worth when they see this movie."

# ᚦᛁᚲ

## Excess Baggage:
## The Truth and the Gossip

THE FIRST MOVIE TO BE PRODUCED BY ALICIA'S OWN production company, First Kiss Productions, is *Excess Baggage*, which she also stars in. Her manager and best friend, Carolyn Kessler, is a coproducer. This movie was originally scheduled for release in January 1997, but it's been pushed back several times. You'll probably see it in theaters sometime in August 1997, after the release of *Batman and Robin*.

This is the first movie to fall under Alicia's multipicture, $10 million deal with Columbia (Sony) Pictures. *Excess Baggage* is a comedy about a wealthy teenage girl (Alicia's character) who tries to get away from her overprotective father (a former CIA operative) by faking her own kidnapping. The problem is, Alicia's character isn't too bright, and just about everyone, including her character's father, discovers that she's behind her own kidnapping. Things get really exciting when Alicia's character actually does get kidnapped, by "Vincent Roche" (Benicio Del Toro), who steals a car while Alicia is in the trunk.

*Excess Baggage* began preproduction in November 1995 and actually started filming in April 1996. Most of the filming was completed by July 1996, before Alicia began work on *Batman and Robin*, but several scenes were reshot later, causing Alicia to have to juggle her production schedule between *Batman and Robin* and *Excess Baggage*.

According to Columbia Pictures' president, Barry Josephson, Alicia was responsible for handpicking her costars in this film, who include: Christopher Walken, Nick Turturro, Harry Connick, Jr., and Benicio Del Toro. "Her instincts about the material have been wonderful," stated Josephson in an interview with the Associated Press. The screenplay was written by Mikhaila Max Adams, an award-winning screenwriter. The screenplay for the movie was purchased by

Josephson after it won at the Austin Heart Film Festival in 1994. Originally, Columbia Pictures allocated a $16 million production budget for *Excess Baggage*. Alicia's salary for the film reportedly made her one of the highest-paid actresses in Hollywood, along with Sandra Bullock.

Associated Press reported that as Alicia's first duty as producer of the film, she wanted to fire herself from the starring role, because she was concerned that her acting would suffer, since she would have to divide her time and efforts between performing and producing. Obviously, Columbia Pictures didn't go for that idea— they wanted Alicia in the starring role. "I'm overwhelmed with it," she told *Entertainment Weekly*. "Every day I put on about fifteen years."

Much of the production for *Excess Baggage* was done in Vancouver, Canada. On some evenings, Alicia is reported to have dropped in at a local nightclub called Richards on Richards. By November 1996, after principal photography on *Excess Baggage* was finished, rumors started floating that Alicia didn't get along with director Marco Brambilla (who also directed *Demolition Man*). In fact, the *Los Angeles Times* reported that one of the film's producers,

David Valdes (who was also executive producer of *In the Line of Fire* and *Unforgiven*),
quit during the film's production, and that
the producers, director, and actors couldn't
agree on whether *Excess Baggage* was actually a comedy or a drama. Producer Bill
Bordon was brought in during production
to replace David.

Also during production, additional comedy writers, including Scott Alexander and
Larry Karaszewski, were hired to incorpo-
rate more comedy material into the script.
Scott told the *Los Angeles Times*, "We're the
guys who have a reputation that we can
find humor anywhere. We liked the trunk
scene, but we wrote another five pages of
trunk material. It's funny if she [Alicia] is in
the trunk and shouting pithy comments to
cast members in the front seat." Rewrites
of the original *Excess Baggage* script were
also done by several other motion picture
writers, including Dick Clement and Ian La
Frenais. Larry has stated that he believes
people not associated with the film are
being far too critical of Alicia's work as a
twenty-year-old producer and actress, especially since they haven't seen *Excess Baggage*. He urges people to give her a shot.

The *Los Angeles Times* quoted one un-
named on-the-set source as saying, "The

fights [between Alicia and Marco] were totally in their faces. It was in front of the entire cast and crew. They fought over dialogue, scenes, script, and even wardrobe. The director would say, 'I'm the director! What are you doing? You have to do this.' She'd be like, 'You don't know anything! You should have read the script before you signed on to it!' Then they would go to their trailers and call their agents. . . . If Marco insisted a scene be played one way, Alicia and Benicio Del Toro would ad lib the way they wanted and refused to do it any other way. To their credit, sometimes it worked."

As production wrapped up on *Excess Baggage* and work began on *Batman and Robin*, Alicia began appearing a lot in the media, and not always too favorably. Reports appeared in several newspapers about her disagreements with director Brambilla, and the September 1996 issue of *Vanity Fair* magazine described Alicia as being too dependent on her manager/friend Carolyn Kessler. During this time, the Hollywood rumor mill also went into overdrive, as totally false stories that Alicia had been replaced by Liv Tyler in *Batman and Robin* began circulating. One rumor implied that Alicia hadn't lost the necessary amount of weight required for her to fit into the Batgirl costume. Another stated that Alicia kept showing up late for work on the movie. The film's director, Joel Schumacher, denied these rumors as production of *Batman and Robin* continued with Alicia portraying Batgirl.

In early November 1996, Alicia popped up in the media once again, this time for striking a sixty-four-year-old male pedestrian while driving her Ford Bronco in Los Angeles. According to police at the accident scene, Alicia was trying to make a left turn when she accidentally hit a man in the crosswalk. No, this isn't the scene in *Clueless* when Alicia blows through a stop sign, or the one where she gets yelled at by her father for getting too many tickets and not having her driver's license. In real life, Alicia does have a driver's license, and since the pedestrian she hit was not hurt badly, and she was not under the influence of drugs or alcohol, she was not cited or criminally charged. The person her car hit was taken to a nearby hospital, where he was treated for neck and shoulder pain and released the same day. Obviously, Alicia only received national publicity for this accident because she is a celebrity, not because she did anything illegal.

On a more positive note, Alicia also received media attention for speaking out in behalf of saving the pigeons (yup, those birds that live in cities). All of Alicia's fans know that she stands up for animal rights, so when a group of celebrities got together to write letters to Pennsylvania Governor Tom Ridge in protest of the state's Hegin Labor Day Pigeon Shoot, an annual event in Schuylkill County, Alicia too wrote a letter. Alec Baldwin, Dennis Leary, Alicia, and other stars threatened to stop filming movies in Pennsylvania if the governor didn't put a stop to the pigeon killing.

So, while not reading reports in the media about Alicia's escapades, you can check out both *Batman and Robin* and *Excess Baggage* in theaters during the summer of 1997.

MEET THE CAST OF *EXCESS BAGGAGE*

The cast of *Excess Baggage*, mainly handpicked by Alicia with the help of casting director Stuart Aikins, features many talented and well-known actors, who gave excellent performances in this movie despite the reported problems on the set. Here's a quick rundown of who costars with Alicia in *Excess Baggage*:

BENICIO DEL TORO, who portrays Vincent Roche, Alicia's boy-toy and a bit of a thug, is a veteran movie actor who has starred in such movies as *Big Top Pee Wee*, *Fearless*, *The Usual Suspects*, and *The Fan*. Off the set, Alicia and Benicio are reported to have become good friends. Like Alicia, during 1995 and 1996 this thirty-year-old actor was constantly working, jumping from one movie project to the next. Alicia told *Premiere* magazine, "I went to see *The Usual Suspects* and I couldn't concentrate on the film, I was so taken by him. . . . He's wonderful to watch. I was pissed off when he died [in the film]." Perhaps it was this performance that convinced Alicia to cast Benicio, who was born in Puerto Rico and raised in Pennsylvania, as her costar in *Excess Baggage*.

NICHOLAS TURTURRO, "Stick" in *Excess Baggage*, is best known as "Detective James Martinez" from ABC-TV's *NYPD Blue*. However, he too has starred in numerous motion pictures and made-for-television movies, including: *Falling from the Sky: Flight 174*, *Jungle Fever*, *Men of Respect*, *Mo' Better Blues*, and *Malcolm X*. It was Nicholas's brother, actor John Turturro (from the movie *Quiz Show*), who persuaded Nicholas to give acting a try. His first role was as an extra in the Spike Lee film *Do the Right Thing*.

Since 1971, CHRISTOPHER WALKEN has starred in about fifty major motion pictures, like: *Last Man Standing, Pulp Fiction, Wayne's World 2, Batman Returns,* and many others. In *Excess Baggage,* Christopher portrays a character named Raymond Perkins.

HARRY CONNICK, JR., is a well-known actor, musician, and composer. You've seen him in *Independence Day* (*ID4*), *Copycat, Little Man Tate,* and *Memphis Belle,* and he composed the music for the film *When Harry Met Sally.* In *Excess Baggage,* Harry's character is "Greg Kistler."

MICHAEL BOWEN previously worked with Alicia in the film *TrueCrime,* which was released back in 1995, so *Excess Baggage* was like a reunion for the two actors. During his career, which so far spans over thirty movies, Michael has worked with many big-name actors, like Eddie Murphy in *Beverly Hills Cop III* and Al Pacino in *Godfather Part III.* In *Excess Baggage,* Michael's character is "Gus."

JACK THOMPSON, who has the honor of playing the father of Alicia's character, is also a veteran movie actor, with over thirty-five movie credits listed on his resume.

Most recently, he portrayed the "Chairman, Joint Chiefs of Staff" in the 1996 block-buster movie *Broken Arrow*.

Other actors featured in *Excess Baggage* include: Robert Wisden ("Sims"), Dean Wray ("Bargemate"), April Telek ("Newscaster"), Brent Stait ("Pilot"), Clair Riley ("Dream Reporter"), Leland Orser ("Barnaby"), Hrothgar Mathews ("Fisherman Cop #1"), Hiro Kanagawa ("Jon"), Matt Huson ("Jogger Cop #1"), and Peter Fleming ("Kayaker").

# seven

# Alicia Wants Her MTV

SINCE THE START OF ALICIA'S CAREER, SHE AND MTV have gotten along just great. After all, she has won several MTV Music Awards for her appearances in the Aerosmith music videos, and then in 1994 she walked away with the MTV Movie Award for "Breakthrough Performance" for her role in *The Crush*. For this award, she beat out Ralph Fiennes (*Schindler's List*), Jason Scott Lee (*Dragon: The Bruce Lee Story*), Ross Malinger (*Sleepless in Seattle*), and Jason James Richter (*Free Willy*).

During that same awards show, Alicia went home with the award for "Best Villain," also for her role in *The Crush*. Once again, she beat some big names, including Macaulay Culkin (*The Good Son*), John Malkovich (*In the Line of Fire*), Wesley Snipes (*Demolition Man*), and T-Rex (*Jurassic Park*).

Also that year (1994), Alicia was nominated for the MTV Movie Award for "Most Desirable Female," but for this award the competition was extremely fierce. She was up against Janet Jackson (*Poetic Justice*), Kim Basinger (*The Getaway*), Demi Moore (*Indecent Proposal*), and Sharon Stone (*Sliver*). Being the youngest nominee for this award, it was obviously something she'd have to grow into. In 1994, the "Most Desirable Female" award went to Janet Jackson, but at the 1996 MTV Movie Awards, it was a totally different story.

The 1996 MTV Movie Awards were filmed in Hollywood while Alicia was busy filming (and producing) *Excess Baggage,* but since she was once again nominated for multiple awards, she took an evening off to attend the show. Alicia arrived at the awards dressed in a blouse and a dark blazer that came from her closet. *TV Guide* described Alicia's outfit as "a Richard Tyler jacket, pants, and an electric blue peekaboo blouse." Her hair was supposed to have been done by famous stylist-to-the-stars Oribe, but a

spokesperson for Oribe reported that a
scheduling error occurred at the last minute
and that Alicia's hair was done by a lesser-
known Los Angeles stylist not associated
with Oribe's salon. Meanwhile, Alicia had
her hair done in an upsweep style that
attracted a lot of positive attention. She
told *TV Guide*, "It's a nightmare to figure
out what to wear for these nights."

When she attended the Academy Awards
a few months earlier, Alicia was dressed in
a Vera Wang gown, and the gossip was that
Alicia looked overweight. Around the same
time, Warner Bros. (the company that produced *Batman and Robin*) hired a trainer
for Alicia (and the rest of the movie's cast),
and she immediately began losing those
excess pounds. To keep in shape, Alicia is
reported to have taken up kickboxing lessons. A spokesperson for Warner Bros.
reported in late April, "She's lost ten pounds,
and she's on her way to losing another ten."
*Batman and Robin* director Joel Schumacher stated that all of the actors involved in
the film are using personal trainers to get
in shape. "They are strenuous roles. They're
roles where the audience gets to know
them a little more intimately physically."
Joel describes the Batgirl costume as "a
skintight version of the Batsuit." The result

of this training and weight-reduction program was that at the 1996 MTV Movie Awards in June, Alicia once again looked absolutely fabulous, and sophisticated—the perfect image for someone who was to take home multiple awards.

The 1996 MTV Movie Awards were hosted by Janeane Garofalo and Ben Stiller, and throughout the two-hour broadcast, which was prerecorded and edited for television, dozens of big-name TV, movie, and recording stars presented awards, performed, and accepted awards for their work throughout the year. This year, the theme of the show was parodies of popular movies. Thus, when it came time to poke fun at *Clueless* and Alicia Silverstone, the cast of TV's *The Golden Girls* (Estelle Getty, Rue McClanahan, and Betty White) were called upon. You haven't seen *Clueless* until you've seen senior citizens portraying hip high school girls from Beverly Hills. Alicia seemed to enjoy the parody (but hey, she was on national television, so she could have been acting).

In 1996, Alicia once again went home with multiple awards—this time for "Best Female Performance" for her role in *Clueless* and "Most Desirable Female." She was also nominated for the "Best Comedic Performance" award, but Jim Carrey won for his portrayal of Ace Ventura in *Ace Ventura: When Nature Calls,* and while *Clueless* was nominated for the "Best Movie" award, that honor went to the movie *Seven.*

During the 1996 MTV Movie Awards broadcast, the award for "Most Desirable Female" was the first to be presented. Claire Danes (*My So-Called Life*) and Shaquille O'Neal announced the nominees—Nicole Kidman, Sandra Bullock, Michelle Pfeiffer, Demi Moore, and Alicia Silverstone—and then presented the award to a rather happy Alicia. She walked onto the stage and during her acceptance speech stated, "Thank you so much. Thank you to MTV, because you guys have been so supportive of me, and [thank you to] all of the MTV viewers. This is a really weird category, and I guess I want to thank the people who are most desirable to me—who are my best friends Brian, Carolyn, Mike, my grandpa, and all of the people who give me love and support, because that's what's desirable. Thank you."

It was Jon Lovitz (*Saturday Night Live*) and Jenny McCarthy (*Singled Out*) who later in the show announced the nominees and presented the award for "Best Female Performance." This time, Alicia's competition included Sandra Bullock (*While You Were Sleeping*), Michelle Pfeiffer (*Dangerous Minds*), Susan Sarandon (*Dead Man Walking*), and Sharon Stone (*Casino*). When Alicia stepped onstage this time, her comments were brief and to the point: "First, I want to thank everyone again, and Paramount for making this movie [*Clueless*]. That was really, really nice of them to see Amy's clear vision. Most of all, I also want to thank Amy Heckerling, whom I don't think I ever really appreciated as much as I do now. I am so happy that I had such a good script to work with, and that you [Amy] stuck to your guns through the whole thing." She also thanked several cast members from *Clueless* by name.

After the awards, Alicia was interviewed by CNN's *Showbiz Today*. During the interview, she expressed how uncomfortable she was having to accept the award for "Most Desirable Female," because she doesn't like how people put so much emphasis on other people's appearance. Alicia stated, "I'm very, very honored that people feel that way, but I just know that I have a very big problem with the way—it's not a big problem, I just think it's sad that there's so much emphasis put on appearance and looks, and this industry is so run by that, and not only the industry, but all of America and all of the world. I mean kids are doing crazy things to themselves to look great and to look like the movie stars look, to look like the models."

Interestingly, actor George Clooney won the 1996 "Breakthrough Performance" award (the one Alicia won back in 1994) for his work in the film *From Dusk Till Dawn*. Just two months after the awards ceremony, George and Alicia began working closely together on *Batman and Robin*.

So, have we seen all that we're going to see of Alicia on MTV? No way! All three of her Aerosmith music videos—"Cryin'," "Amazing," and "Crazy"—continue to air regularly on MTV. Meanwhile, as long as Alicia is hard at work making new movies, chances are she'll be nominated again and again for MTV Movie Awards in the future. In interviews, however, Alicia admits that she doesn't watch MTV. "I don't have time! I've been working so hard," she says. Alicia does add, however, that she enjoys listening to music from many different artists. Alanis Morissette, Prince, Sinead O'Connor, and David Gray are among her favorite recording artists.

# *eight*

## Acting Takes Training

ALICIA TAKES HER JOB AS AN ACTRESS VERY SERI-
ously, which means she is always striving
to improve her skills. Whenever she has
time, Alicia participates in acting classes
and workshops in order to perfect her
acting abilities. Between the ages of twelve
and fifteen, she was a student in Judi
O'Neil's acting workshops. Later in her
career, she participated in one of the world's
most prestigious acting workshops at Shakespeare & Company.

Based in Lenox, Massachusetts, Shakespeare & Company offers intense workshops and training to a highly select group
of professional actors and actresses from

stage, movies, and television. The training offered at Shakespeare & Company explores many elements of acting, such as voice and movement, Elizabethan dance, fight and physical violence for the stage, and Shakespeare's texts. Alicia, like many serious actors and actresses, has a strong love of Shakespeare's work, and while she hasn't yet performed any Shakespeare on stage, the skills she learned at Shakespeare & Company have helped her in all of her acting projects—from comedies like *Excess Baggage* to action-oriented roles like Batgirl in *Batman and Robin*.

Alicia knows that being a successful actress in the long term will depend on more than having a pretty face and a youthful appearance. Thus, Alicia is using the acting training she received at the workshops to prepare herself for a lifelong career as a well-respected and skilled actress.

Dennis Frausnick is the director of training at Shakespeare & Company, and one of the people responsible for Alicia's training when she participated in the intense acting workshops offered by this highly prestigious acting school. "Alicia really loves working on Shakespeare. We offer training for actors who already have professional acting experience. The majority of the people who participate in our workshops are highly experienced actors and directors. We run two-month-long intensive workshops which offer a complete immersion into personal training. While the workshop is in session, the days begin at eight A.M. and often go until ten P.M. The workshops are extremely challenging, both physically and emotionally, for all of the participants. We stretch people in every direction at the same time, which is one of the reasons why the actors, like Alicia, who complete the workshop find it so invigorating."

The Month-Long Intensive Workshop that Alicia completed is designed for adult actors, and Alicia learned about it from actress Christine Lahti, with whom she costarred in *Hideaway*. (Christine portrayed Lindsey Harrison, the mother of Alicia's character.) "Alicia already had over nine movie and television roles on her resume, and she knew she had some free time that she wanted to use to study acting. Alicia felt that if she didn't take serious acting lessons, she would be beyond her depth," according to Dennis. "As an actress, she knew that trading on her youth would be a limited thing that would eventually run out, and she wanted the training. Shakespeare & Company offers a safe environment for Alicia to work in, and one in which she would have some anonymity. Nobody would pay attention to the fact that she was a star, so she could focus her energies on learning."

When Alicia contacted Dennis about participating in the Month-Long Intensive Workshop, his immediate reaction was not to admit her because of her young age. "I don't allow people under the age of twenty to participate in this workshop. However, I spent a lot of time on the phone talking with her manager before I finally accepted Alicia into the program. If she hadn't already had the amount of work that she did on her resume, I wouldn't have accepted her. In speaking with her manager, she assured me that Alicia was very serious about studying Shakespeare, and that Alicia was capable and willing to work hard throughout the program."

You're probably wondering why an actress who is already making megabucks starring in commercially successful movies with the biggest names in Hollywood would spend time studying Shakespeare. As Dennis explains, "The demands when performing Shakespeare are so strong for accuracy that studying Shakespeare opens you up physically, vocally, and emotionally as an

actor or actress. Performing Shakespeare
is so difficult that after you're able to do it,
all other acting roles seem very easy. Professional runners train for a marathon by
running over many hills and practice on
the toughest terrain possible, so that when
they actually run a marathon it seems easy
by comparison. Performing Shakespeare
well is considered to be one of the most
difficult achievements for an actor or actress. Because Alicia has a love of Shakespeare's work, I know that she really wants
to perform his work onstage at some point
in the future."

Dennis says that Alicia is a very instinc-
tual actress. "She has wonderful instincts.
Film work, however, never prepares actors
and actresses to use language as language.
The camera is so close when filming movies,
the acting is very physical, and the actor uses
just about everything else but the words.
Onstage, the opposite is true, especially
with classical material, like Shakespeare,
where everything has to come through the
words themselves. Learning to use language was something that Alicia worked on
during the workshop, and is something
that will be a valuable skill for her throughout her acting career. Alicia came to the
workshop with a respect for Shakespeare

but not a strong firsthand knowledge of his work. She had watched the movies that have been made based on his work, and she knew that all of the actors and actresses that she had respect for aspired to do Shakespeare. I think she really wanted to know why that was. From participating in the workshop, Alicia learned to use herself differently as an actress. She already knew acting techniques for film work, but like everyone in her position, she had to go back to square one and learn about acting for the stage."

During the time that Alicia was involved in the workshop, her schedule was more hectic than a movie production schedule. "Every morning breakfast is from seven-thirty A.M. to eight-fifteen A.M. Immediately after that, the day's first class, called Physical Awareness, began. This was a warm-up class that helps to get the participants focused. At nine-fifteen A.M., everyone broke up into small groups for a voice class. From eleven A.M. to twelve-thirty P.M. each day was a movement class. In both the voice and movement classes, the actors and actresses were trained in how to stay attuned, alert, aware, and relaxed. The students must learn not to make things happen, but to allow them to happen. After lunch, between one forty-five P.M. and four forty-five P.M., everyone participated in either a three-hour study of Shakespeare's texts or in two ninety-minute classes in movement and stage fighting. In the evenings, the actors did scene work and spent hours discussing theater and why we do the things we do as actors. The day ends around ten P.M., sometimes later," says Dennis. "Each day, everyone is also required to spend at least thirty minutes writing personal journal entries about their experiences of the day."

By working as her acting coach and teacher, Dennis quickly discovered what so many other people who have worked with Alicia have, which is that she is extremely mature for her age and very responsible. "I found that she was one of the most professional people in the workshop. There were many things that Alicia hadn't yet experienced or didn't know because of her age, but the way that she dealt with things was absolutely as a professional. She was wonderful to work with."

After having taken the Month-Long Intensive Workshop, Alicia returned to Shakespeare & Company to perform a staged reading of a Maureen Hunter play. "We were going to try to fit the show into our calendar so that she could return again and perform the play for a long run. This would be the next step in her training—to actually log stage time—but because of her busy schedule working on *Excess Baggage* and then immediately beginning work on *Batman and Robin,* she couldn't dedicate the time necessary during our 1996 season to participate in a full stage production. Since completing the workshops, Alicia and I have stayed in contact. Whenever I'm in Los Angeles, we'll meet for lunch and discuss whatever role she is currently working on. For each acting role that she accepts, Alicia spends time carefully preparing. She treats herself like she's in training all the time, so she continues to learn and grow as an actress. Alicia is one of the nicest people I have ever met. She is a lovely person to spend time with. She is totally unpretentious, and worked extremely well with everyone at Shakespeare & Company. I sincerely hope I'll have the opportunity to work with her on a theatrical production in the future."

To Alicia, Dennis offers the following advice: "Don't get sucked up into the Hollywood image thing. You can expend far more energy than it's worth trying to become someone you're not in order to meet the demands of other people. The kinds of judgments that are made within the industry are really destructive, and actresses like Alicia have to be able to seal themselves against it, and know that it has nothing to do with their real talent."

Alicia was quoted in the August 1995 issue of *Vanity Fair* magazine as saying, "Shakespeare is my god now, completely in every way. He is a religion in his own. I think he was a genius." While participating in the workshop, Alicia said, "Every day we have to walk up this long hill to class. It's so beautiful you want to hold hands with someone. . . . There's so much to learn, it's mind-boggling."

One of the programs Shakespeare & Company offers to young, nonprofessional actors and actresses is called Shakespeare & Young Company. This is a summer program for those between fifteen and twenty years old that offers a mix of classes and actual performance work. If you're serious about acting and want to follow in Alicia's footsteps, you can find out more about the Shakespeare & Young Company program by writing to: Shakespeare & Company, The Mount, P.O. Box 865, Lenox, MA 01240-0865.

Every year, over forty thousand theatergoers from around the world visit the Berkshires in Massachusetts to attend one of the more than three hundred fifty performances of about twenty different theatrical productions done by Shakespeare & Company. You can bet that someday soon, Alicia will be the star of at least one of these productions.

# NINE

## Alicia Speaks Out for the Animals

IN *CLUELESS*, CHER'S CHARACTER IS CONSTANTLY accused by her stepbrother, Josh, of being shallow and self-centered. Do you remember this scene?

### JOSH:
"Actually, I'm going to a Tree People meeting. We might get Marky Mark to plant a celebrity tree."

### CHER:
"How fabulous. Getting Marky Mark to take time from his busy pants-dropping schedule to plant trees. . . . Josh, why don't you just hire a gardener?"

**JOSH:**

"You know, maybe Marky Mark wants to use his popularity for a good cause and make a contribution. In case you've never heard of that, a contribution is the—"

**CHER:**

"Excuse me, but I have donated many expensive Italian outfits to Lucy, and as soon as I get my license, I fully intend to brake for animals. And I have contributed many hours to helping two lonely teachers find romance."

**JOSH:**

"Which I'll bet serves your interest more than theirs. You know, if I ever saw you do anything that wasn't ninety percent selfish, I'd die of shock."

**CHER:**

"Oh, that would be reason enough for me."

Cher is a character in a movie, but Alicia does in fact use her popularity for a good cause and to make a worthwhile contribution. Many of Hollywood's biggest stars work closely with their favorite charities in order to use their fame to help raise awareness and money for the causes that interest them. For as long as she can remember, Alicia's passion has been animals.

In an interview with Hollywood OnLine, Alicia stated, "If people admire my work and admire me, hopefully they'll admire what I believe in. What I believe in is protecting animals in a major way. My mom and I are going to open a foundation eventually to help the animals. I feel like if my voice is heard, I can express just how important it is for young people to stop being selfish and really look at how important animals are. It's not young people's fault; it's the adults that don't respect animals and honor them. Animals are everything. They give so much more than humans to the earth, and I think that it is extremely important to love, respect, and honor them. I don't think that's done a lot. I hope that my voice will be helpful in raising awareness. At one point when I was a little girl, I thought that I was going to save all of the animals in the world. That was my thought, but I didn't know how I was going to do it because nobody was going to listen to me. Now people listen to me, and that's good."

In many interviews, Alicia refers to her

dog Sampson as one of her very best friends.
"He's gorgeous! He's the best-looking man I
know! I found him on the street, so I don't
know his birthday. He's so spoiled," she
told a group of fans during a chat on
America Online.

One of the things Alicia has done to help
animals is to work with the Ark Trust, Inc.,
a nonprofit organization devoted to raising
public awareness about the many animal-
protection issues facing us today. The Ark
Trust was established in 1991 and is the
only animal rights group whose primary
focus is to facilitate progressive coverage of
animal issues by the major media. In order
to do this, the organization works closely
with writers, reporters, and producers from
newspapers, magazines, radio, and television in order to educate the public, influence social attitudes, and encourage changes
in behavior leading to a more humane and
compassionate society.

Every year, one of the ways the Ark Trust
captures the attention of people throughout the country is to produce the Genesis
Awards television special. Broadcast on The
Discovery Channel, this awards program
collects and evaluates how animals are
depicted in movies, television, print, music, and art. This awards ceremony honors

individuals in the entertainment and news media. The 1996 Genesis Awards was hosted by talk show host Leeza Gibbons and *NYPD Blue* star Dennis Franz. Throughout the awards show, which was filmed in Beverly Hills in front of a 1,200-person audience, dozens of celebrities, including Alicia Silverstone, presented awards.

The award that Alicia was responsible for presenting at the 1996 Genesis Awards was for "Outstanding Feature Film." Out of the dozens of actors and actresses invited to participate in the awards show, Alicia was the youngest. To introduce Alicia, Leeza Gibbons stated, "Since her appearance on the Genesis Awards last year, she has become one of the most dependable spokespeople for this cause." Dennis Franz added, "She has also become one of Hollywood's hottest properties. She is young and she's beautiful. . . . Please welcome Alicia Silverstone."

Alicia then walked out onstage wearing a lovely formal black dress. Her hair was at shoulder length, partially covering her right eye. She read a prepared speech announcing the winner of the "Outstanding Feature Film" award, then presented the award to the producers and stars of the motion picture *Babe*.

If you want to find out more about this charity that Alicia is so fond of, you can write to: The Ark Trust, Inc., 5461 Noble Avenue, Sherman Oaks, CA 91411-3519.

Throughout the year, Alicia also works with a nonprofit organization that's based in Beverly Hills called Last Chance for Animals. This group is dedicated to ending animal suffering wherever it may occur—in the laboratory, on factory farms, in the fur industry, and in "entertainment." Last Chance for Animals is involved in many different programs designed to protect all types of animals. The group offers workshops to teach people how to keep their own pets from getting stolen, and campaigns for government legislation to protect animals from unnecessary medical experimentation and to prevent stolen animals from being used for experimentation.

Every year the group holds two special events—World Week Against Vivisection (the week of April 24) and National Pet Theft Awareness Day (February 14). These events are attended by many Last Chance for Animals supporters from around the country, including Alicia Silverstone when she's available to participate.

According to a spokesperson for Last Chance for Animals, Alicia has become

involved with the group because of her
concern for all animals. She has attended
several of the group's special events, and
often talks about the group's work in interviews. In addition, any fan who writes
Alicia a letter and requests an autographed
photo will often receive the photo accom-
panied with information about Last Chance
for Animals, or information about what
Alicia's fans can do to protect their own
pets and the animals in their community.

In many areas of the country, pet theft
has become a serious problem. Last Chance
for Animals offers these suggestions for
keeping your pet safe:

- Keep your pet indoors, especially when
  nobody is home.

- Make sure your dog always wears identification and has a license. Have your
  dog or cat registered. Ask your veteri-
  narian about some of the ways you can
  protect your dog by tattooing it or in-
  serting a microchip into your pet.

- If you have a pet cat, keep it inside at all
  times. Research shows that the average
  "outdoor cat" only lives 2.5 years.

- Keep your dog on a leash when walking
  it.

- Spay or neuter your pet—"fixed" pets are less likely to stray from home.

- Take photos of your pet in case you need them for identification if it disappears.

- Never tie your dog outside of a store or restaurant while you go shopping, and never leave your pet locked in your car with the windows closed.

- If you put your pet up for adoption, first visit the place where it will be living.

You can find out more about what you can do to help protect animals by calling Last Chance for Animals at (800) 4-PET-THEFT, or by writing the group at: 8033 Sunset Blvd., Suite 35, Los Angeles, CA 90046.

# *ten*

## Cybersurfing for Alicia on the Web

THE INTERNET IS A WORLDWIDE NETWORK MADE UP of thousands (perhaps millions) of computers. Together, these computers offer an amazing amount of information on just about anything and anyone . . . including Alicia! In fact, Alicia has become one of the most popular celebrities in cyberspace.

Fans of Alicia from all over the world who are also computer buffs have created Web sites dedicated to their favorite young actress. In fact, there are over fifty Web sites located around the world that offer pictures, news, interviews, and gossip about Alicia and her movies. The majority of these sites on the Web were created and are maintained by her fans. Because these sites are maintained by fans, they are *not* officially sanctioned by Alicia, and the info offered on these unofficial sites isn't always 100 percent accurate—so beware of gossip!

To access the Internet's World Wide Web, you're gonna need a computer and a modem (which is a gadget that allows a computer to communicate with other computers over telephone lines). You'll also need access to the Internet, which can be done by subscribing to one of the popular on-line services (such as America Online, CompuServe, or the Microsoft Network); or you can obtain access to the Internet's World Wide Web directly from a local service provider in your city. Oh, and if you don't happen to own a personal computer, no problem—many schools and colleges offer Internet access so students can "surf the net." You can also visit your local library or one of the "cyber cafes" that are popping up across America. Cyber cafes allow you to pay by the hour to surf the net while munching on snacks.

Anyway, once you're on-line, here's how to find the many World Wide Web sites on the Internet that contain info about Alicia. First, access a Search Engine (such as

Yahoo!—**http://www.yahoo.com**). When asked for a keyword to search, type in "Alicia Silverstone" or the name of one of her movies—(*Clueless*, etc.). This will provide you with an up-to-date list of Web sites that contain Alicia-related information.

This chapter contains a partial listing of Alicia-related Web sites. If you're a fan of the movie *Clueless*, you'll want to start your cybersurfing adventure at the official *Clueless* Web site that's sponsored by Paramount Pictures. The address for this site is: **http://www.paramount.com/Clueless. html.** At this exciting site, you'll find photos, info about the sound track, and the scoop on the movie's stars. There's also a *Clueless* videocassette site based in Europe which you can access at this address: **http://wwwZ.paramount.com/homevideo/ b/index.** The official site for *Hideaway* can be found at: **http://www.hollywood.com/ movies/hideaway/.**

Columbia Pictures, the company that released *Excess Baggage,* has a Web site you can visit at this address: **http://www.spe. sony.com/pictures/index.html.**

For the latest news on *Batman and Robin,* be sure to visit the official Warner Bros. Web site at **http://www.movies. warnerbros.com**.

If you think you're the only Alicia Silverstone fan, then you're the one who's clueless. A bunch of her truly dedicated fans have created their own Web sites in order to share their love and admiration for her. Remember, all of these sites were developed by fans of Alicia, which means they're less permanent than corporate-sponsored sites. So, if you receive an error when trying to access one of the following Web sites, simply try another one.

Let's take a quick tour and see what a few of these sites have to offer to Alicia-holics. . . .

## THE ALICIA SILVERSTONE INTERNET MAILING LIST

In addition to World Wide Web sites, there's also a mailing list that you can subscribe to via E-mail. To join an Alicia-related mailing list on-line (it's totally free), send an E-mail message to: **alicia-fans-request@xmission.com.** Within the body of the message, and as the message subject, type the word "subscribe." Once you send this E-mail, you'll start receiving E-mail messages from fellow Alicia fans, and be able to participate in Alicia-related conversations on-line. The topics her fans talk about vary greatly. For example, fans might discuss their favorite hairstyle from a movie Alicia has appeared in, and then vote whether they prefer her with long hair or short. People also post comments about their favorite movies of Alicia's. Another way to subscribe is to send an E-mail message to **majordomo@xmission.com**, and to type in the body of the message "subscribe alicia-fans your@ address."

There's another Alicia-related Internet mailing list you can subscribe to by sending an E-mail message to: **list@midnight. org.** In the body of your message, write "JOIN Alicia." To access a third Alicia-related Internet mailing list, send an E-mail message to: **alicia-fans-request@list.best. com**, and within the message write the word "subscribe."

*The Adorable Alicia Silverstone Site—*
http://www.globalxs.nl/home/d/dcnco

This exit off the Information Superhighway brings you to a Web site that's jampacked with cool features and beautiful pictures. Here you'll find a biography of Alicia, quotes, images (tons of cool pictures), reprints of magazine articles about her, audio clips from Alicia's movies, and video clips from her movies and music videos. This is one Web site that no Alicia fan should miss!

*Alicia Silverstone—*
http://rohan.sdsu.edu/home/almilli/alicia/alicia.html

Since this site was created in August 1995, well over 220,500 people have visited it. It offers photos of Alicia, a bio, and plenty of information about her various movies.

*Batman and Robin* opened in theaters in June 1997; however, America got a sneak peak at Warner Bros.' official two minute and twenty-eight second movie trailer on *Entertainment Tonight* and on the Internet in late February. To check out the official *Batman and Robin* web site for yourself (which is separate from the Warner Bros. web site), here's the address: http://www. batman-robin.com.

**http://us.imdb.com/search** (search the database for Alicia Silverstone)
**http://www.alicia-silverstone.com**
**http://www.ior.com**
**http://www.nashville.com/~alicia**

http://www.pingnet.ch/shung/alicia

http://www.geocities.com/SoHo/1781/
alicia.html

http://www.xmission.com/~bbray/Alicia

http://www.erols.com/rdignan/brian/
alicia.htm

http://www.duke.edu/~csa3/AliciaOpen.
html

http://users.aol.com/batgirljnr/alicia.html

http://www.ior.com/~compubra/alicia/

http://www.geocities.com/hollywood/
8442

http://ra.nilenet.com/~laforce/alicia.
html

http://rohan.sdsu.edu/home/almilli/
alicia/alicia.html

http://pages.prodigy.com/Nirvana/
pipeline/Alicia.html

http://www.wolfe.net/~heydrick/alicia.
html

http://users.aol.com/burton9999/alicia.
html

http://svendsen.res.wpi.edu/alicia.html

http://www.glue.umd.edu/~kgold/Alicia.
Silverstone.html

http://www.geocities.com/Hollywood/
6488/alicia.html

http://www.nd.edu:80/~rchung/

http://www.mindspirng.com/~sabotaged/
zerodog.htm

**http://www.geocities.com/hollywood/7973/
asmain.htm**

**The Internet Movie Database—
http://www.moviedatabase.com
Mr. Showbiz—http://www.mrshowbiz.com**

*Additional Alicia Web Sites (Based Around the World)*

France—**http://www.isg.fr/hp/David.Sok/
alicia/alicia.html**
The Netherlands—**http://www.noord.bart.
nl/~jellew**
Australia—**http://ww.ecn.net.au/alicia**
Canada—**http://www.geocities.com/
Hollywood/Hills/3395/index.html**

*The Alicia Silverstone Internet Newsgroup*

Newsgroups are yet another way fans of
Alicia can communicate with each other.
To join the Alicia USENET Newsgroup (it's
also free), you can subscribe to **alt.fan.
alicia-slvrstone,** if your Internet service
provider allows you to subscribe to newsgroups. (All of the major on-line services,
including America Online, the Microsoft
Network, Prodigy, and CompuServe, allow
you to subscribe to newsgroups if you're
a member.) Other newsgroups you might

want to join are: **alt.fan.teen.starlets**, **alt. binaries.pictures.teen-starlets**, and **alt. binaries.pictures.celebrities**.

Topics discussed in the newsgroup are similar to the E-mail messages fans post on the Alicia Silverstone Internet mailing lists. Here's your opportunity to go on-line and meet other Alicia fans from around the world.

*Other Places Alicia Fans Can Visit in Cyberspace*

For the latest gossip and entertainment news, Hollywood OnLine (**http://www. hollywood.com**) offers an up-to-the-minute resource for movie buffs. The television series *Extra*, which often does stories about Alicia, runs a Web site at this address: **http://www.extratv.com**, and to see what *Entertainment Tonight* has to say about Alicia, visit *ET*'s forum on the Microsoft Network (on the Internet, the address is: **http://et.msn.com/**.)

As mentioned earlier, just about everyone who loves Alicia's work knows she has won a bunch of MTV Movie Awards. To see pictures of her at the various MTV Awards shows, visit MTV's forum on America On-line (keyword: MTV).

# 𝒬𝓊𝒾𝓏

## How Well Do You Know Alicia?

HERE'S A QUICK QUIZ TO DETERMINE HOW WELL YOU know Alicia Silverstone. Getting a perfect score on this quiz won't boost your grades in school, nor will it make you a smarter person. It will, however, prove how much of an Alicia fan you really are. So, like—are you ready to begin?

1. In what city was Alicia born?

    a) New York
    b) Denver
    c) Los Angeles
    d) San Francisco

2. How old was Alicia when she starred in her first TV commercial?

   a) 12
   b) 13
   c) 14
   d) 15

3. What company was her first television commercial for?

   a) Pizza Hut
   b) Domino's Pizza
   c) McDonald's
   d) Burger King

4. Alicia has won all of the following awards, except:

   a) "Best Actress Ever"—Academy Awards
   b) "Most Desirable Female"—1996 MTV Movie Awards
   c) "Best Actress, Motion Picture"—American Comedy Awards
   d) "Best Villain"—1994 MTV Movie Awards

5. Alicia currently has a multifilm production deal with Columbia Pictures. What's the name of her production company?

a) Romance Productions
b) Silverstone Productions
c) First Kiss Productions
d) Passion Productions

6. What TV series did Alicia turn down a starring role in?

a) *Party of Five*
b) *Beverly Hills, 90210*
c) *Melrose Place*
d) *Friends*

7. What did Alicia name her dog?

a) Snoopy
b) Fido
c) Sampson
d) Sonny

8. For what movie did Alicia win MTV's "Breakthrough Performance" and "Best Villain" awards?

a) *Clueless*
b) *The Crush*
c) *Hideaway*
d) *TrueCrime*

9. What is the name of Cher's father in *Clueless*?

a) Mel Hamilton
b) Wendell Hall
c) Scott Rudin
d) Alan Friedman

10. Growing up, where did Alicia spend many of her summers?

a) France
b) England
c) Beverly Hills
d) Palm Springs

11. What is the first movie Alicia both starred in and produced?

a) *Excess Baggage*
b) *Hideaway*
c) *TrueCrime*
d) *Clueless*

12. In *Batman and Robin,* Alicia costarred with everyone but . . .

a) Arnold Schwarzenegger
b) George Clooney
c) Chris O'Donnell
d) Adam West

13. In what music group's videos did Alicia appear?

a) Aerosmith
b) Snoop Doggy Dog
c) Prince (or the Artist Formerly Known as Prince)
d) Nirvana

14. In the movie *Scattered Dreams*, Alicia portrays a character named Phyllis Messenger. In what decade does the movie take place, and in what state does the Messenger family live?

a) 1960s, Florida
b) 1950s, Florida
c) 1950s, South Carolina
d) 1960s, South Carolina

15. In how many music videos has Alicia appeared?

a) 1
b) 2
c) 3
d) 4

16. In the movie *Clueless*, how did Cher's mother die?

a) During heart transplant surgery
b) During a routine liposuction procedure

   c) She got run over by a car that Dion
      was driving
   d) Of natural causes

17. What recording artist or music group
does *not* perform on the *Clueless* sound
track?

   a) Radiohead
   b) Coolio
   c) Beastie Boys
   d) Aerosmith

18. How old was Alicia when she became
emancipated and earned her high
school equivalency diploma (G.E.D.)?

   a) 14
   b) 15
   c) 16
   d) 17

19. In what movie did Alicia costar with
Jared Leto (*My So-Called Life*)?

   a) *Hideaway*
   b) *TrueCrime*
   c) *The Babysitter*
   d) *Cool and the Crazy*

20. Who is Alicia's costar in the movie
*TrueCrime*?

a) Kevin Dillon
b) Matt Dillon
c) Paul Rudd
d) Jeff Goldblum

21. What music group and/or movie star provided the background music for Alicia's TV public service announcement that was produced by PETA?

a) Dogstar and Keanu Reeves
b) Madonna
c) The Monkees
d) Coolio

THE ANSWERS:

1) d    2) c    3) b    4) a    5) c

6) b    7) c    8) b    9) a    10) b

11) a    12) d    13) a    14) b    15) c

16) b    17) d    18) b    19) d    20) a

21) a